LUCY WEBB HAYES:
A FIRST LADY BY EXAMPLE

(A VOLUME IN THE
PRESIDENTIAL WIVES SERIES)

OTHER BOOKS IN THE
PRESIDENTIAL WIVES SERIES
Robert P. Watson, Editor

Dolley Madison
Paul M. Zall
2001. ISBN: 1-56072-930-9
(Hardcover)
2001. ISBN: 1-56072-937-6
(Softcover)

A "Bully" First Lady:
Edith Kermit Roosevelt
Tom Lansford
2001. ISBN: 1-59033-086-2
(Hardcover)
2011. ISBN: 978-1-61761-845-1
(Softcover)

Sarah Childress Polk, First Lady
of Tennessee and Washington
Barbara Bennett Peterson
2001. ISBN: 1-59033-145-1
(Hardcover)
2002. ISBN: 1-56072-551-1
(Softcover)

Frances Clara Folsom Cleveland
Stephen F. Robar
2002. ISBN: 1-59033-245-8
(Hardcover)
2004. ISBN: 1-59454-150-7
(Softcover)

Edith Bolling Galt Wilson:
The Unintended President
James S. McCallops
2002. ISBN: 1-59033-556-2
(Hardcover)
2011. ISBN: 978-1-61761-846-8
(Softcover)

Lucretia
John Shaw
2002. ISBN: 1-59033-349-7
(Hardcover)
2004. ISBN: 1-59454-151-5
(Softcover)

Jackie Kennedy:
Images and Reality
Mohammed Badrul Alam
2003. ISBN: 1-59033-366-7
(Hardcover)
2011. ISBN: 978-1-61761-840-6
(Softcover)

Eliza Johnson: Unknown
First Lady
Jean Choate
2004. ISBN: 1-59454-097-7
(Hardcover)

Caroline Lavinia Scott Harrison
Anne Chieko Moore
2004. ISBN: 1-59454-099-3
(Hardcover)
2009. ISBN: 978-1-60456-271-2
(Softcover)

Lou Henry Hoover: A Prototype for First Ladies
Dale C. Mayer
2004. ISBN: 1-59033-806-5
(Hardcover)
2011. ISBN: 978-1-61761-841-3
(Softcover)

Lucy Webb Hayes: A First Lady by Example
Russell L. Mahan
2004. ISBN: 1-59454-011-X
(Hardcover)
2011. ISBN: 978-1-61761-843-7
(Softcover)

Betty Ford: A Symbol of Strength
Jeffrey A. Ashley
2004. ISBN: 1-59033-407-8
(Hardcover)
2004. ISBN: 1-59454-149-3
(Softcover)

Dutiful Service: The Life of Mrs. Mamie Eisenhower
Robert E. Dewhirst
2004. ISBN: 1-59454-007-1
(Hardcover)

Grace Coolidge: Sudden Star
Cynthia D. Bittinger
2005. ISBN: 1-59454-473-5
(Hardcover)

Texas Bluebonnet: Lady Bird Johnson
David Murphy
2005. ISBN: 1-59454-556-1
(Hardcover)
2006. ISBN: 1-60021-259-X
(Softcover)

Nancy Reagan: The Woman Behind the Man
Pierre-Marie Loizeau
2004. ISBN: 1-59033-759-X
(Hardcover)
2011. ISBN: 978-1-61761-844-4
(Softcover)

Nancy Reagan in Perspective
Pierre-Marie Loizeau
2005. ISBN: 1-59454-695-9
(Softcover)

Ellen A. Wilson: The Woman Who Made a President
Sina Dubovoy
2007. ISBN: 1-59033-791-3
(Hardcover)
2011. ISBN: 978-1-61761-782-9
(Softcover)

Jackie Kennedy – Trailblazer
Mohammed Badrul Alam
2007. ISBN: 1-59454-558-8
(Softcover)

LUCY WEBB HAYES:
A FIRST LADY BY EXAMPLE

(A VOLUME IN THE
PRESIDENTIAL WIVES SERIES)

RUSSELL L. MAHAN

Nova Science Publishers, Inc.
New York

For permission to use material from this book please contact us:
Telephone 631-231-7269; Fax 631-231-8175
Web Site: http://www.novapublishers.com

NOTICE TO THE READER

The Publisher has taken reasonable care in the preparation of this book, but makes no expressed or implied warranty of any kind and assumes no responsibility for any errors or omissions. No liability is assumed for incidental or consequential damages in connection with or arising out of information contained in this book. The Publisher shall not be liable for any special, consequential, or exemplary damages resulting, in whole or in part, from the readers' use of, or reliance upon, this material.

Independent verification should be sought for any data, advice or recommendations contained in this book. In addition, no responsibility is assumed by the publisher for any injury and/or damage to persons or property arising from any methods, products, instructions, ideas or otherwise contained in this publication.

This publication is designed to provide accurate and authoritative information with regard to the subject matter covered herein. It is sold with the clear understanding that the Publisher is not engaged in rendering legal or any other professional services. If legal or any other expert assistance is required, the services of a competent person should be sought. FROM A DECLARATION OF PARTICIPANTS JOINTLY ADOPTED BY A COMMITTEE OF THE AMERICAN BAR ASSOCIATION AND A COMMITTEE OF PUBLISHERS.

Full color presentation of graphics is available in the E-book.

LIBRARY OF CONGRESS CATALOGING-IN-PUBLICATION DATA

Mahan, Russell L.
 Lucy Webb Hayes : a First lady by example / Russell L. Mahan.
  p. cm. -- (Presidential wives series)
 Includes bibliographical references and index.
 ISBN 978-1-61761-843-7 (softcover : alk. paper) 1. Hayes, Lucy Webb, 1831-1889. 2. Hayes, Rutherford Birchard, 1822-1893. 3. Presidents' spouses--United States--Biography. I. Title.
 E682.1.H39M34 2010
 973.8'3092--dc22
 [B]
                                        2010037367

Published by Nova Science Publishers, Inc. ✦ New York

CONTENTS

FOREWORD

Robert P. Watson

The old saying that "behind every successful man is a woman" is perhaps nowhere more evident than in the White House. Even a cursory examination of the wives of presidents reveals a group of remarkable individuals who made many contributions to the lives and careers of their husbands, the presidency, and even the nation. Over the course of U.S. history first ladies have presided over state dinners, overseen extensive historical renovations of the Executive Mansion, held press conferences, campaigned for their husbands, testified before Congress, championed important social causes, and addressed the United Nations.

As a candidate for the presidency speaking of the role his wife would assume in his administration Bill Clinton stated that when the public elects a president, they are getting "two for the price of one!" To an extent such a statement has always been true. First ladies have been a viable part of the presidency since the nation's founding. Of the men who served as president during the country's history, nearly all of them served with a first lady at their side. Only a handful of presidents have held the office without their spouses. For instance, both Andrew Jackson and Chester A. Arthur had lost their wives prior to their presidencies; Rachel Jackson dying in the interim between her husband's election and his inauguration and Ellen Arthur just prior to her husband's Vice Presidency. The wives of both Thomas Jefferson and Martin Van Buren passed away years before their presidencies. But they were exceptions. Only two bachelor presidents have been elected, Grover Cleveland and James Buchanan, however the former married while in office. Three presidential wives died while serving in the White House:

Letitia Tyler, Caroline Harrison, and Ellen Wilson. However, both President John Tyler and President Woodrow Wilson later remarried while in office.

Presidential wives have served without pay and, until very recently, often without proper recognition. So too have they wielded political power and social influence despite the fact that they are neither elected nor appointed. In part because they are not elected or accountable to the citizenry and in part because of strict social conventions that precluded women from participating in politics for much of the nation's history, presidential wives have been forced to exercise their power and influence in a behind-the-scenes manner. Yet, in this capacity many wives have functioned as their husband's trusted confidante and private political advisor.

Presidential wives have faced great challenges, not the least of which include the loss of privacy and specter of assassination looming for themselves and their families. The presidency is arguably the most demanding job in the country and the challenges of the office are experienced by the president's family. Amazingly, several first ladies served while trying to raise a family. Presidential wives have faced severe scrutiny, an invasive press corps and curious public, and criticism from journalists and the president's political enemies. This is perhaps one of the experiences that all first ladies have shared. Not even popular wives like Martha Washington, Abigail Adams, or Jacqueline Kennedy were spared from harsh personal attacks.

The first ladyship has been the "unknown institution" of the White House. For most of its history it has been ignored by scholars and overlooked by those studying national and presidential politics. However, this is slowly changing. The public, press, and scholars are beginning to take note of the centrality of the first lady to the presidency. A new view of the president's spouse as a "partner" in the presidency is replacing more traditional views of presidential wives. Even though the Founding Fathers of the country gave no thought to the president's wife and the Constitution is silent concerning her duties, today the "office" has become a powerful, recognized institution within the presidency, complete with staff and budgetary resources that rival the so-called "key" presidential advisors.

It is also an intriguing office whose occupants are no less fascinating themselves. Indeed, the presidential wives are a diverse lot that includes new brides barely out of their teens to grandmothers who had spent a lifetime married to men that would become president. There have been women of refinement and wealth and there have been wives who would seem ill-prepared for the challenges of the White House. And of course, there have been successes and there have been failures.

The first ladyship is one of the nation's most challenging and dynamic public offices. So too is it an office still in development. In the words of First Lady Barbara Bush, concluding her remarks when delivering the commencement speech at Wellesley College, "And who knows? Somewhere out in this audience may even be someone who will one day follow in my footsteps, and preside over the White House as the President's spouse. I wish *him* well!"

In the volumes of this Series the reader will find the stories of women who fashioned the course of American history. It is the goal of the publishers and myself that this book and each volume in the Presidential Wives Series shed light on this important office and reveal the lives of the women behind the American presidency.

I hope you enjoy this book and the entire Series!

Robert P. Watson, Series Editor

PREFACE

Rutherford B. Hayes and Lucy Webb Hayes lived their lives as though they knew Rutherford would become President of the United States one day. They not only led exemplary lives from beginning to end, but saved an incredible amount of information for the future historian. Lucy saved almost all of her letters since girlhood. Rutherford did likewise, plus kept a regular diary from his youth to his death.

It is the opinion of this author that it is more interesting to hear the story of Lucy Hayes through the words of Lucy and those who knew her, when their statements are clear and succinct, than to have the events filtered through a historian's paraphrase and summary. Accordingly, there is a fair amount of quotation from Lucy herself, from Rutherford, and from others, in the course of this book. It is hoped that these quotations have been woven into the biography in such a manner as to give the reader a closer view of its subject than can he had by pure narrative.

It is necessary to write about Rutherford to know what Lucy was doing. This is true for two reasons. First, he left an excellent diary which records many events for which no writing from Lucy or others is available. Second, even without the diary, it is impossible to understand the life of a First Lady without also knowing something of the life and career of the man who took her to the White House. Still, this biography is about Lucy Hayes, not Rutherford.

Thanks must be extended to several parties. I happily state my appreciation to my wife, Kami Mahan, for her support and encouragement. I give my thanks to Professor Robert P. Watson who believed in me and invited me to write this book. It could not have been written without the information and resources made available by Nan Card and the staff of the excellent Rutherford B. Hayes

Presidential Center Library in Fremont, Ohio. Appreciation is also given to Nova Science Publications for publishing the Presidential Wives Series, and including my work within it.

Russell L. Mahan

Chapter 1

THE PRESIDENTIAL INAUGURATION

Lucy Webb Hayes was in a terrible uncertainty on March 1, 1877, as she prepared to go to Washington, D.C., for the presidential inauguration. The administration of Ulysses S. Grant was ending but the American presidential selection process had so far failed to choose a successor. With just three days to go in Grant's term, it was not definitely known whether her husband, Rutherford B Hayes, or his Democratic opponent, Samuel J. Tilden, would be sworn in as President of the United States. As a result, Lucy did not know whether she would become the presidential wife and hostess or the unofficial position would go vacant, as Tilden was a lifelong bachelor. It was believed by most informed people that Hayes would very soon be selected as the winner by the Electoral Commission, which had been appointed by the Congress to resolve the controversial election, but nothing is certain in politics until it actually happens.

As the returns came in on the evening of the November 1876 presidential election, it was apparent that the Republican Hayes had lost, and that Tilden had become the first Democrat since James Buchanan twenty years before to win the presidency. Surrounded by family, friends and supporters, the results were awaited in the Hayes' Cincinnati home. When the reports of voting came in from around the country, and it was evident that it was not going well, Lucy retired to her bedroom early with a bad headache, a physical torment with which she was on familiar terms. Rutherford came in to console her, then returned to the disconcerted friends in the parlor. Lucy, however, stayed in her room.

Later they would learn that the election was not decided after all. Perhaps Rutherford had not lost after all. He had indeed lost the popular vote by 4,284,757 to 4,033,950,[1] but under the United States Constitution the President is chosen by the electoral college, not the popular vote. With 185 electoral votes necessary to win, the count was 184 for Tilden and 165 for Hayes. Another twenty electoral votes from Florida, Louisiana, Oregon and South Carolina were disputed. Political battling went on for week after week, with accusations of corruption, rumors of cheating and threats of political revolt flying in all directions. It was unfortunate that the 1876 election, in the year of the American centennial, was such a debacle.

At Rutherford's instruction, one incident during this time of stress was not reported to the public. It would only have made things worse. As the Hayes family was in their Cincinnati home at the hour of the evening meal, a bullet crashed through their front window, traveling through a parlor and an open door and into the wall of the library. After that son Webb Hayes began carrying a pistol with him at all times to protect his father.[2]

Amidst it all, Rutherford was a model of calm and self-possession. He personally was prepared to win or lose, and said and did nothing to agitate the situation. But now in March it was believed that the Republican majority on the Electoral Commission would, in the end, find that all twenty electoral votes should be cast for the Republican candidate. It would have to be so for Hayes to win.

Now, as the Hayes family made its journey, the final outcome was still uncertain, but time for traveling to Washington, D.C., for the inauguration was running out. They could wait no longer if they were to be available for the ceremony in the event that Rutherford was the one selected. Although they thought it likely that Rutherford would win, they also knew they just might be returning home in a few days as private citizens. The bags were packed and the children were made ready. The evening before departure there was a reception at the State House in Columbus, as Ohio bid farewell to its Governor.

At this moment in time, Rutherford was 54 years old, and Lucy 45, both in the prime of middle age. They had been married for twenty-four years, during which time eight children had been born. Birchard was 23 and in his last year of law school at Harvard University, where his father had attended before him. Webb would be twenty-one later that month, and he was chosen by his father to fill the magnificent position of being the President's "unofficial" personal secretary. Rud (Rutherford) was 18 and going to Cornell University in Ithaca, New York. Fanny, the only girl, was nine years old, and young Scott had just turned six. Two sons,

---

[1] William A. Degregorio, The Complete Book of U.S. Presidents, Fort Lee, New Jersey: Barricade Books, Fort Lee, New Jersey, 2001, p. 286.
[2] H. J. Eckenrode, *Rutherford B. Hayes: Statesman of Reunion*, New York: Dodd, Mead & Company, 1930., p. 235.

Joseph and George, had been born during the Civil War but died separately before their second birthdays. Just two years ago, Manning Hayes had died on Lucy's birthday, also before his second birthday. Rutherford, Lucy, Webb, Fanny and Scott were now heading for the nation's capital for the adventure of a lifetime.

Local college cadets in Columbus provided the prospective First Family with a courtesy escort to the train station, and a large crowd surrounded them there The Hayes family, with its entourage, boarded two special train cars that had been furnished to them, which were attached to the regular passenger train bound for the nation's capital.

More crowds awaited the train at each city, town and rural junction as it worked its way through Ohio. "The enthusiasm was greater than I have seen in Ohio before," Rutherford wrote appreciatively in his diary.[3] Finally, the excited family went to sleep for a few hours. When the train neared Harrisburg, Pennsylvania, at dawn the next morning, the sleepy riders were awakened to be told the news that Congress had just made an official and final count of the electoral votes. Rutherford B. Hayes was selected as President by a vote of 185 to 184. As the inevitable result, Lucy Webb Hayes would be First Lady of the United States. The men in the presidential party began to cheer, prompting Hayes to calm them with, "Boys, boys, you'll waken the passengers."[4]

Samuel Tilden graciously accepted the verdict of defeat, or at least he did so in public. Considering the circumstances, it is not too much to say that this was a heroic action. Tilden then deserved, and still deserves, a nation's thanks for his willingness to accept the outcome of the political process, adverse though it was to his own and his party's interests. The manner in which the presidential contest was resolved was not America at its finest. Many dissatisfied people said that the election had been stolen, and dubbed the new President as "Rutherfraud B. Hayes." Tilden could at his word have created an unprecedented crisis by calling his supporters to arms. There was considerable talk of just this very thing, but he would have no part of it. He instructed his followers to stop their struggle, and instead consoled himself with his victory in the vote of the people. "I can retire to private life," he said, "with the consciousness that I shall receive from posterity the credit of having been elected to the highest position in the gift of the people, without any of the cares and responsibilities of the office."[5]

---

[3] Charles Richard Williams, Editor, *Diaries and Letters of Rutherford B. Hayes*, Columbus, Ohio: Ohio State Archeological and Historical Society, 1922, (hereinafter cited as "Diary") March 14, 1877.
[4] William Seale, *The President's House*, Washington, D.C.: The White House Historical Society, 1986, Volume 1, p. 488.
[5] Degregorio, p. 285.

The contest was finally over, the anxious waiting was ended, and Rutherford would in fact be President in two days. Surely, as the train clicked down the miles of track, Lucy Hayes contemplated what lay ahead for him and herself. Her life would be changed forever.

She probably thought of the letters she had received in recent weeks. As it became apparent that Hayes would likely win the election, people from across the land began to write Lucy. Without any act on her part, she became an object of hope for many thousands, perhaps millions, of her fellow Americans. Letters began to come in, imploring her to advance one cause or another, urging her to use her expected influence in the direction the writer wished to see. The way Americans now viewed Lucy Hayes was stated by Rosa E. Hartwell in a letter to Lucy from the Women's Christian Temperance Union in Washington. "In a few days we hope to welcome to our Capital your husband as the chief Ruler of our nation," Hartwell wrote, "and to you the wife of the chief Ruler... not alone as his wife; but as the one who, we trust, will wield a powerful influence...."[6]

People asked Lucy Hayes to wield that anticipated influence to advance various social causes. She was asked to stop the tradition of dances at presidential inaugural balls,[7] to not serve wines in the White House,[8] and to stop polygamy in the West. Some just wanted her photograph, or for her to write back. Such responses would be a prized possession of the owner to have and show around.

Other letters she had received promoted not a grand social cause, but rather the personal prospects of the writer. John Curry Miller wrote a song entitled *Grand Columbia: An American National Song*, which he sent to Lucy "with the desire that you will bring it to the attention of Mr. Hayes." This, Miller candidly hoped, "will so favorably dispose of you toward the author that it will secure him...suitable employment."[9] This was the quintessential office seeker, the great irritator of all previous Presidents. M. A. Shropshire, the mother of a girl who went to school with Lucy, came right to the essential point. "I want President Hayes to give my boys an office," she unabashedly announced, "that will be respectable and will give us a competency."[10] A man wanted to work on the White House staff;[11] the widow of a Methodist minister wanted to work in the household.[12]

---

[6] Letter to Lucy Hayes from Rosa E. Hartwell, dated February 28, 1877, Lucy Hayes Papers, Rutherford B. Hayes Presidential Center Library (hereinafter cited as "Papers").
[7] Letter to Lucy Hayes from an anonymous sender, dated February 28, 1877, Papers.
[8] Letter to Lucy Hayes from Harriet Stevens Whitemarsh, dated February 20, 1877, Papers.
[9] Letter to Lucy Hayes from John Curry Miller, dated February 19, 1877, Papers.
[10] Letter to Lucy Hayes from M. A. Shropshire, dated February 24, 1877, Papers.
[11] Letter to Lucy Hayes from Z. L. Hough, dated February 27, 1877, Papers.
[12] Letter to Lucy Hayes from Mrs. Rev. J. Jennings, dated February 27, 1877, Papers.

Other correspondents simply said they were praying for her, something which was undoubtedly appreciated by the religious Lucy. The letters that were most endearing, however, were probably those of her former classmates at the various girls' schools she had attended over the years in Chillicothe, Delaware and Cincinnati. Numerous women, who in former years had known the young Lucy, wrote to her with congratulations and remembrances.

At about 9:30 later that Friday morning the train pulled into the station in Washington, D.C. Senator John Sherman of Ohio and his brother, General William T. Sherman, greeted the President-elect and his family, and escorted them to the Senator's home, where they would stay until they moved into the White House.[13] As a portent of things to come, a crowd gathered at the station and cheered the family as they arrived. Life would now be very different for the Hayes family.

After breakfast Rutherford went to the White House with Senator Sherman to call on the President. Ulysses Grant had invited the President-elect's family to stay at the White House, but the offer was declined. The Hayes would come for dinner on Saturday, but would otherwise stay with the Shermans. There was a certain tension between the Grant and Hayes families. When Rutherford left the governorship in 1872, Ulysses had offered him only the very minor position of assistant U.S. treasurer in Cincinnati. This was so insignificant a post that Lucy felt offended. Out of politeness, however, it was not mentioned now by anyone.

Under the Constitution the second term of President Grant expired on March 4th, which in 1877 happened to fall on a Sunday. When this had happened in the past, Presidents James Monroe in 1821 and Zachary Taylor in 1849 had decided against a public ceremony on the Sabbath. Monroe took the oath privately on the appointed day, then held the public inaugural ceremony the next day. Taylor simply let the country go without a President for a day, waiting until the fifth to take the oath.

Rutherford also did not want to be inaugurated on the Sabbath Day, so a public ceremony was scheduled for Monday, the fifth. Secretary of State Hamilton Fish was concerned about an interruption of presidential tenure if there was no swearing in prior to the expiration of Grant's term. With whisperings of possible trouble over the election results, he felt it would be safest for there to be a President at every moment, without a gap of any kind. "I did not altogether approve but acquiesced,"[14] Hayes recorded in his diary. Being prudent under the unusual circumstances and taking wise counsel, Rutherford was quietly sworn in

---

[13] Diary, March 14, 1877.
[14] Ibid.

as President of the United States in the Red Room of the White House on the
evening of Saturday, March 3rd, prior to the dinner honoring the Hayes family.
Nobody thought to bring a Bible to the meeting, so a search was made until one
was found. Rutherford was given the oath of office by Chief Justice Morrison R.
Waite in the presence of Grant, Grant's son Ulysses Jr., and Fish. Lucy was not
present.

There was a little banter at the Saturday state dinner between Lucy Hayes and
Julia Grant. Julia loved being the wife of the President, and therefore the social
queen of Washington, and did not want to leave the White House. She was
extremely unhappy when Grant followed the two-term tradition established by
George Washington and followed by all of this successors to that point, and
refused to run for re-election to a third term.

A detectable snippiness arose when Lucy invited Julia to the inauguration.
"No," said Julia, "I have already witnessed two inaugurations." When Lucy asked
if the Grants would vacate the White House during the ceremony, Julia shot back,
"No...I am not."[15] The outgoing hostess had decided to have a post-inaugural
luncheon, the first of its kind, in honor of the incoming President. Then, with the
clock more than expired on her husband's presidency, she would give up the
President's Mansion at the last possible moment.

The nation looked, as it always did, with anticipation upon the incoming
President. What kind of a leader would be prove to be? How would be change
things in Washington? What would his family be like? Rutherford was honest and
steady, a likeable person who enjoyed friendships and meeting new people. Lucy
was a good match for him. She was sunny in her disposition and in her preference
for weather. She was optimistic, accepting the good that people did without
feeling the need to search behind their actions for improper motives. She did not
like the company of nay sayers. Where Rutherford was more serious, she was
lighter. Where he was less religious, she was more so. They complimented and
balanced each other in a way that worked out for a lifetime.

On Monday, March 5th, the public event was held. An estimated thirty
thousand people were in attendance. Inaugural day was fairly cold at thirty-five
degrees at noon. The skies were cloudy with periodic snow,[16] and the people were
wearing heavy coats. Custom and the weather required gloves and hats as well.

The new Vice President, William A. Wheeler, was sworn in first. In the
tradition of that political day, the presidential nominee did not select his running

---

[15] Carl Sferraza Anthony, *First Ladies: The Saga of the Presidents' Wives and Their Power*, New
York: William Morrow & Company, 1990, p. 224.
[16] "The Weather of Inauguration Day" by Patrick Hughes, 1968, for the National Oceanic and
Atmospheric Association.

mate. Although three Vice Presidents had succeeded to the highest office within the last thirty six years, the men selected for the position were chosen for reasons other than their qualification to be President of the United States. Most people didn't even know who he was, including Rutherford. When Wheeler was first mentioned for the vice presidential nomination several months earlier, Rutherford wrote to his wife, asking, "I am ashamed to say, Who is Wheeler?"

At the time of his selection it may have been hoped that Wheeler would bolster the image of the Republican ticket for incorruptible leadership, which it may have actually done to a small degree. Also, it may have been hoped that Wheeler would help win the vital state of New York for the Republicans, but this hope was dashed when the Democratic Party nominated New York Governor Samuel Tilden to run against Hayes. Tilden was the one who carried New York.

William Wheeler was a New York Congressman known among his colleagues for both incorruptibility and frequent timidity. In what was known as the "Salary Grab" by Congress in 1873, Wheeler voted against a fifty per cent pay raise and $5,000.00 in back pay, evening going so far as to return the $5,000.00 when the bill passed. He was something of an odd person, declining to campaign during the election and writing in a letter that "I regret that I was nominated. You know I did not want the place." He said he would rather be Speaker of the House of Representatives than "laid away" as Vice President.[17]

The presidential swearing-in ceremony was held on the East Portico of the Capitol Building. An estimated thirty thousand people were in attendance. An official announced "the President of the United States" and those in the seats fell silent and arose to their feet as President Grant and President-elect Hayes walked in together. Mrs. Grant was present after all, and was in the company of Lucy, Fanny and Scott. Lucy "was intensely absorbed, but composed in manner," wrote Eliza Davis, a lifelong friend who witnessed the event. Rutherford and Lucy "were both outwardly serene during this ceremonial scene, and so remained throughout the reading of the inaugural before the great sea of upturned faces in the square of the Capitol."[18]

The President-elect spoke to the crowd, but in the age before microphones only a small portion of those in attendance could hear and understand what was said. Rutherford then raised his hand and was sworn in (again) as President of the United States by Chief Justice Waite of the Supreme Court. The new President then kissed the Bible, which was open to the first eleven verses of the 118th

[17] Mark O. Hatfield, *Vice Presidents of the United States, 1789-1993*, Washington, D.C.: U.S. Government Printing Office, 1997.
[18] Eliza Davis, *Lucy Webb Hayes: A Memorial Sketch*, Cincinnati: Cranston & Stowe, 1890, p. 30.

Psalm.[19] Rutherford B. Hayes was a religious man, and the place where the Bible was opened was surely something he intended. Perhaps he had opened it to this page because of verses 5 and 6, which read: "I called upon the Lord in distress: the Lord answered me, and set me in a large place. The Lord is on my side; I will not fear: what can man do unto me?"

In his address President Hayes spoke of the problems before the nation. He discussed the need to bring the Southern states back fully into the Union, and to treat the former slaves equally with their former masters. He called for the reform of the civil service to eliminate the never-ending curse of office seekers, for a single presidential term of six years, and for the continuance of isolation from European affairs. Most of all, he called for national unity after a Civil War and a divisive election. His most notable statement was, "He serves his party best who serves his country best." The presidential term of Rutherford B. Hayes was now underway.

Lucy was prominently on hand at the inauguration, with her two youngest children, Fanny and Scott, on either side of her. She was dressed in the plain but dignified way she always dressed, without jewelry, not attempting in any way to compete with the fashionable Julia Grant or Mary Lincoln. Her hair was severely parted down the center, with a comb at the back, a style she kept all her life. She was 5'4" tall and somewhat overweight. She was completely comfortable being herself.

Not all eyes at the inaugural ceremony were on the President. Some were watching Lucy Hayes, wondering what sort of person she would be in the White House. Most who observed her were favorably impressed with the woman, her education, and her prospects as the wife of the Chief Executive.

By 1877 there was something new in the nation's capital, a trend that had developed after the Civil War - women journalists, turning out stories not only for women's magazines and newspaper columns, but also for hard political news. It was only natural that they would focus on the wife of the President. Among these was Mary Clemmer Ames. She was the author of a column called "A Woman's Letter from Washington," which appeared in *The Independent* of New York City. She was favorably impressed with the new President's wife, and described her as the "First Lady." This was one of the first, though not the very first, uses of the term. However, following this occasion the term generally increased in public usage.

In the dramatic and romanticized prose of the day, Ames wrote: "Meanwhile, on this man of whom every one in the nation is thinking, a fair woman between

---

[19] Diary of James A. Garfield, March 5, 1877.

two little children looks down. She has a singularly gentle and winning face. It looks out from the bands of smooth dark hair with that tender light in the eyes which we have come to associate always with the Madonna. I have never seen such a face reign in the White House. I wonder what the world of Vanity Fair will do with it? Will it frizz that hair? - powder that face? - draw those sweet, fine lines away with pride? - hide John Wesley's [Methodist] discipline out of sight, as it poses and minces before *the first lady of the land?*"[20]

Ames observed that Lucy was as "strong as she is fair." "All that I know," she concluded, "is that Mr. and Mrs. Hayes are the finest looking type of man and woman that I have seen take up their abode in the White House."[21]

Another newspaper was far less favorable. "Mrs. Hayes is in no sense of the word a pretty woman," the *Cincinnati Commercial* uncharitably wrote. "She never could have been pretty, but she was and is fine looking - striking, rather than handsome.... She is not elegant, in society phrase, but she is well bred, and has a heartiness of manner quite refreshing on Washington."[22] Just what is meant by being fine looking and striking but not pretty or handsome is unclear.

First Ladies, of course, are not sworn into any office and make no inaugural speeches, but they nonetheless enter upon a tenure of administration in the White House. During the living memory of those alive in 1877, the wives of the Presidents had been widely varied in their personal nature, just as their husbands were. In the last fifty years, two Presidents (Andrew Jackson and Martin Van Buren) were widowers and one (James Buchanan) a bachelor. Three of the wives had no interest whatever in being First Lady (Anna Symmes Harrison, Margaret Smith Taylor and Eliza McCardle Johnson), and Lucretia Christian Tyler was too ill to fulfill any role and soon died. Abigail Powers Fillmore was frequently ill and often let her daughter fulfill the role of hostess. Two others (Jane Appleton Pierce and Mary Todd Lincoln) suffered from mental problems. Julia Gardiner Tyler and Sarah Childress Polk of the 1840s, and Julia Dent Grant of the 1870s, had been the most active presidential wives. There was an anticipation by Washington society of what sort of presidential hostess Lucy Hayes would be.

There was no traditional inaugural parade or ball held in 1877 because there was no time in which to plan them. After all, no one knew for sure who the President would be until it was too late to put something together. Lucy had been implored by one letter writer to forego the event anyway because of its serving of alcohol, but Lucy had nothing to do with the lack of a ball. There was a luncheon afterward, however, as planned by Mrs. Grant. It was a large event attended by

---

[20] New York *Independent*, scrapbook news clippings, Papers.
[21] Ibid.
[22] Cincinnati Commercial, April 8, 1877, scrapbook news clippings, Papers.

Supreme Court Justices, Congressmen, Senators, the diplomatic corps, and other dignitaries. At the conclusion, Julia, fighting back tears, publicly said to Lucy, "Mrs. Hayes, I hope you will be as happy here as I have been for the past eight years."[23] She got into the carriage with her husband, and when the door closed, she burst into tears.

Some celebration did take place, however. Lucy and Rutherford attended a reception at Willard's Hotel. "In the evening the streets of Washington were so thronged with people that it was difficult to move about except with the general mass," the *Harper's Weekly* reported. "All the public buildings and many private homes were brilliantly illuminated. Bands were playing, rockets flying, and cannon firing. Pennsylvania Avenue from end to end was one sea of light."[24] An estimated ten thousand lantern bearers marched down Pennsylvania Avenue, singing Republican campaign songs. They ended their parade on the White House grounds, where fireworks were shot into the night sky.

When it was all over, Congressman James A. Garfield wrote in his diary that "[t]here were many indications of relief and joy that no accident had occurred on the route for there were apprehensions of assassination."[25] Federal troops had been brought into town. Six secret service agents had trotted alongside the carriage conveying Presidents Grant and Hayes, but nothing happened. It is ironic that just a little more than four years later it would be Garfield who would be assassinated in Washington by a political discontent, in the very train station in which the Hayes family had arrived.

"At the close of this wonderful day," remembered Eliza Davis, "we gathered round the dinner table in the White House, where for the first time Mrs. Hayes assumed the duties of hostess. Perhaps she was a little subdued, but, with that exception, she was her usual self, considerate, cheerful, watchful of the comfort of everyone." Afterward she called the guests around her and said that while all the guest rooms were excellent, one was par excellence. So no one would be offended by seeing another assigned to the room, she had the guests draw straws to see who would get the State bedroom.[26]

That Monday night, as they retired to bed after an incredible day, Rutherford and Lucy were surely exhilarated at their first night in the White House. So very few people in a hundred years of American history had reached that place of such high esteem. The greatness of some of those few was both inspiring and

---

[23] Anthony, p. 224.
[24] Ari Hoogenboom, *The Presidency of Rutherford B Hayes*, Lawrence, Kansas: University Press of Kansas, 1988, pp 55-56.
[25] *Ibid.*, p. 55.
[26] Davis, 1890, p. 35.

humbling. What did the future hold for them? As she rested her head on a pillow, perhaps Lucy pondered in her mind how a fatherless young girl from Chillicothe, Ohio, had ended up as the First Lady of the United States.

Chapter 2

THE EDUCATION OF A YOUNG WOMAN

Cholera is a disease of the small intestines, which in the nineteenth century struck quickly and could kill within hours. One of the last diary entries of President James K. Polk, who died from it, wrote that he had "a derangement of stomach and bowels."[1] It originated in India and was present there for centuries, but remained a local problem until 1817. It then began to spread through Turkey and Russia and into Europe, finally reaching England. In the middle of 1832 it came with passengers on ships, touching America for the first time. The terrible epidemic of disease and death which ensued in the United States became a major factor in the life of Lucy Ware Webb.

In the summer of 1833 Dr. James Webb left his young family in Chillicothe, Ohio, and journeyed home to Lexington, Kentucky, where his father was ailing and the family was preparing to free some slaves. When he bid farewell to his wife, Maria, and their three young children, Joseph, James and Lucy, ages six, five and not quite two, those left behind did not know that they would never see him again. While in Kentucky, the 38-year-old doctor contracted the dreaded cholera that was raging across the state. Maria received word that he had been stricken and departed at once to be with him, but he was gone before she could get there. Dr. Webb, his father, his mother and his brother, all died during the epidemic.[2]

Born on August 28, 1831, Lucy Ware Webb was almost two years old at the time of her father's death. She never really knew him, and she grew up fatherless. She was fortunate, however, in that her mother's father, Isaac Cook IV, took the

---

[1] Diary of James K. Polk, March 25, 1849.

family under his aging wing and sustained them for several years. He had been an early settler in the area, and had been a judge and member of the state legislature. He was a widower, his wife Margaretta having died the same year as Dr. Webb.

Lucy spent her early years in the town of Chillicothe, named from an Indian word meaning "principal town," in the central part of southern Ohio. It had been founded in 1796, and was the state's first capital city when Ohio was admitted to the Union in 1803. It was a center of farming and trade. Her grandfather Cook and her father had made their careers there.

In those days there was the beginning of a social cause proclaimed by a growing number of people across the country which was known as "the temperance movement." It was the reformist response of many people to the chronic problem of alcoholism in American society. Drunkenness, then as now, led to personal addiction, ruined lives, failure at work, broken homes, unsupported families, and a host of other ills. The curse was widespread across the nation. The temperance movement was an effort to fight these problems by education, personal abstinence from alcohol, encouraging abstinence in others, restrictions on the sale of liquor, and even its total prohibition by law. Not all temperance advocates supported prohibition. In 1846 Maine became the first state to enact total prohibition, and though the movement rose and fell over the decades, national prohibition was eventually enacted in 1920 by the eighteenth amendment to the United States Constitution. It was repealed thirteen years later by the twenty-first amendment.

Lucy's grandfather, Isaac, was a strong advocate of the temperance movement. He had once had whiskey shipped to his home by the barrel, but his observation of the debilitating effects of liquor on people, along with his religious conversion to Methodism, caused him to change his mind on the subject. He became convinced of the evils of alcohol to the point that he became a frequent spokesman against it, joining actively in the movement.

One of the devices used by the reformers to encourage people not to indulge in alcohol was the pledge of abstinence. This was usually done with a printed card, which would typically have a statement such as, "I agree to abstain from the use of all intoxicating liquors as a beverage." Isaac Cook urged all of his grandchildren to sign a personal pledge, and Lucy, who sincerely believed alcohol to be an evil in society, signed one of these cards. She honored that pledge all of her life, and as a result, she never suffered from the debilitating afflictions that

---

[2] Emily Apt Geer, *First Lady: The Life of Lucy Webb Hayes*, Fremont, Ohio: The Rutherford B. Hayes Presidential Center, 1995, p. 4.

often accompany alcohol. Years later, however, she would pay a political price for this stand.

While riding through a storm to speak at a temperance meeting, Isaac Cook became severely chilled. It developed into pneumonia, and he died in 1844 at the age of seventy five. Losing a father figure for the second time in her young life, Lucy was still just twelve years old.

Maria Webb, widowed at only twenty eight years of age, kept her family of two boys and a girl together through difficult years. The extent of her husband's fortune was sufficient to sustain her and the children in a comfortable though not extravagant lifestyle for the remainder of Maria's life. She was helped in business affairs by her father, and after his death by her brothers, particularly Scott Webb.

Maria had inherited from her husband fifteen to twenty slaves, who were across the Ohio River in the salve state of Kentucky. Part of her husband's visit there was for the purpose of arranging for freeing them and sending them back to Liberia on the west coast of Africa. Some family friends suggested that Maria would be wise to sell the slaves for the cash to be gained from the transaction. Maria, a fervent abolitionist, answered that "before I will sell a slave, I will take in washing to support my family."[3]

Education was highly valued in the Webb family. Despite her widowed status Maria made it a point to have all of her children educated far in excess of the tradition of the times. This was unusual in itself, but even more unusual because it included her daughter, Lucy. She attended public schools in the area, including the Chillicothe Female School.

After the death of her father in 1844, Maria moved the family to Delaware, Ohio, a town of about two thousand people twenty miles north of the Ohio capital city of Columbus. The reason for the move was to place her sons in Ohio Wesleyan College, a United Methodist Church school that had been founded just two years before. Maria bought a home near the college campus, which became a gathering place for her three children and their many college friends. Lucy also attended the school, but young women were not permitted to officially enroll in the college department of that school. She was, however, permitted to attend some classes informally. In 1846 she wrote to her aunt that she was taking algebra, chemistry and Latin and that the studying "comes hard at first." She closed the letter by mentioning what would become a common theme fore her, that "I am not very fond of letter writing."[4] In this, she never changed.

---

[3] Diary, November 18, 1883.
[4] Letter from Lucy to "Aunt," dated September 18, 1846, Papers.

It just so happened that Delaware, Ohio, was the home town of a young man named Rutherford Birchard Hayes. He had been born there in 1822, so he was nine years older than Lucy. At the time the Webbs moved there, Rutherford was attending Harvard Law School in Cambridge, Massachusetts. The Hayes family, however, had moved on to live in Columbus, but often visited their former home. Sophia Hayes, Rutherford's mother, met Maria Webb, and was favorably impressed with her fifteen year old daughter. She soon thought of her favorably in connection with her own unmarried son, who was often called "Rud."

Rutherford had been born into a well-to-do family and had the best money education could buy. He was sent in early teens to a preparatory school in Connecticut, then attended the exclusive Kenyon College in Ohio, finally going back to Massachusetts to Harvard Law School. Notwithstanding this, he had an unpretentious nature, free from haughtiness. He was open, mild mannered, engaging and friendly.

Upon graduation, Rutherford established a law practice in Lower Sandusky, later called Fremont, where his uncle Birchard Hayes lived and could steer clients to him. Lucy and Rutherford shared a very important bond in common, for he, too, grew up fatherless. His own father, named Rutherford Hayes, Jr., had been a prosperous merchant in the state of Vermont and then in Delaware, Ohio. At the age of thirty five he contracted a disease and died suddenly, eleven weeks before the birth of his namesake son.

The emptiness created by this loss was filled to a considerable extent by Sophia Hayes's bachelor brother, Sardis Birchard. After some unreliable younger years, Sardis settled down to become an extremely reliable man who was the most successful businessman in the Lower Sandusky area. It was Birchard who paid for Rutherford's education, set him up in law practice, fronted his early expenses, gave fatherly guidance, and in later years gave money for a house in Cincinnati and built a mansion he call Spiegel Grove as a summer home for Rutherford and his family. He was a solid mainstay in Rutherford's life. More than that, Sardis and Rutherford had a familial love and a genuine attachment to each other.

Rutherford Birchard Hayes was a serious young man, full of ambition and a desire to do something good with his life. "I will put down a few of my present hopes and designs for the sake of keeping them safe," he wrote in his diary when he was eighteen and ready to go out into the world. "I do not intend to leave here until about a year after I graduate, when I expect to commence the study of law. Before then I wish to become a master of logic and rhetoric and to obtain a good knowledge of history. To accomplish these objects I am willing to study hard, in which case I believe I can make, at least, a tolerable debater. It is another intention of mine, that after I have commenced in life, whatever may be my ability or station, to preserve a reputation for honesty and benevolence; and if ever I am a public man I will never do anything inconsistent with the character of a true friend and good citizen. To become such a man I shall necessarily have to live in accordance with the precepts of the Bible, which I firmly believe, although I have never made them strictly the 'rule of my conduct.'"[5] These vows, made at a young age, were kept by the man throughout his life.

In matters of romance and courting, developments can take interesting turns. Had earlier plans worked out, Fanny G. Perkins would have been First Lady of the United States instead of Lucy W. Webb. Fanny was a young lady from a prominent and historical family in New London, Connecticut, whom Rutherford met in 1846 while she was visiting relatives in Ohio. He had "a sort of presentiment that she is probably for me."[6] He followed her back to Connecticut and proposed marriage, and she accepted. However, they soon lapsed into a quarrel over whether to live in Connecticut or Ohio, and Rutherford boarded the train for home without her. She later married someone else and moved to Ohio anyway.[7] The other fellow never did become President of the United States.

In the fall of 1847 Maria enrolled Lucy in the Wesleyan Female College in Cincinnati, Ohio. The institution was perfect for Maria - it was Methodist based, it offered post secondary education for girls, and it was modest in cost. It was here that the sixteen year old Lucy would receive her advanced education, thereby becoming the first First Lady to receive a college degree.

Wesleyan Female College had been established in1812 but the portion dedicated to college for women had not opened until thirty years later. "The school is very large numbering about three hundred and forty," Lucy wrote. "They have lately built a new school house. It is three stories having on each of the lower floors six rooms [and] the third is nearly all taken up in the chapel. It is a very nice building."[8] Lucy lived in an adjacent boarding house, which was also had three storeys. She and a roommate shared a small room with a bed, table and a washstand. She received a well rounded education there, probably studying rhetoric, mathematics, geology, music, painting, French, German and English, among other things.[9]

That same fall Rutherford was living in Lower Sandusky, attempting to get a law practice started. "I wish I had a wife to take charge of my correspondence

---

[5] Diary, June 19, 1841
[6] Harry Bernard, *Rutherford B Hayes and his America*, New York: The Bobbs-Merrill Company, Inc., 1954, p.154.
[7] Degregorio, p. 282.
[8] Letter from Lucy to Uncle J. J. Cook, dated February 18, 1848, Papers.
[9] Geer, p. 13.

with friends and relatives," he wrote humorously to his mother. "Women of education and sense can always write good letters but men are generally unable to fish up enough entertaining matters to fill half a sheet." Knowing of the conspiring of his mother concerning Lucy Webb, he teased her about it. "By the by, I hope you and Mother Lamb will see to it that Lucy Webb is properly instructed in this particular," he said in jest. "I am not a-going to take a wife on recommendation unless her sponsors will fulfil to the utmost what they assume. Don't forget now."[10] The subject turned to be an ironic one, as years later, Rutherford turned out to be the one to keep up the family correspondence, not the disinclined Lucy.

A week later he wrote another letter to his sister, Fanny. "I remember my thoughts matrimonial-wise of a year since," he said, referring to his near-bride, Fanny Perkins, "but have no very fixed notions on the subject now. Mother in her letter to Uncle [Sardis Birchard] says she thinks the choice she made at Delaware is not just the one. Well, I am content to go on or stop as she prefers." The 25-year-old continued on speaking of the 16-year-old girl, "If Lucy is too young she must find me an older one. Youth, however, is a defect that she is fast getting away from and may perhaps be entirely rid of before I shall want her."[11]

The light hearted teasing was still going on the next summer. "I see you have converted Fanny to your good opinion of Lucy W.," Rutherford wrote his mother in 1848, "except the freckles, and she says they may be washed out. Never mind about faults only skin-deep. I can easily forgive such, not being at all fastidious in matters of that sort. Uncle and Pease have made a[nother] choice for me here [in Lower Sandusky]. There are many points about their selection which would please you, some that please me, and a very few that Fanny would like. As I must suit you all, our Sandusky girl will hardly catch me at present."[12]

Lucy Webb was a good student in her three years of college at Wesleyan from the fall of 1847 to the early summer of 1850. She was elected during her last year to the Young Ladies Lyceum, which was considered an honor. On the night of January 5, 1850, Rutherford B. Hayes visited her at the school, and he was thereafter a frequent visitor. Lucy graduated in June of 1850 with a liberal arts degree, a rare event for young women of the middle of the nineteenth century. She delivered a speech at her graduation which she entitled "The Influence of Christianity on National Prosperity."

The text of that speech has been preserved. She began by mentioning that all peoples everywhere worshiped a god of some kind, but that through ancient

---

[10] Diary, October 16, 1847.
[11] Diary, October 23, 1847.
[12] Diary, June 18, 1848.

history only the Jews were free from idolatry. Otherwise ignorance and superstition prevailed in the world. "[T]here should be a system of worship which would inculcate pure morals, a right feeling for others, and regard to the rights and wishes of neighboring nations." Christianity is the religion to do this. "Our own country also is an example of the prosperity attending nations who have cast aside the gods the heathen.... Let Christianity be banished from our land and this fair republic would be dashed from the high position which it has reached...." She concluded with these words: "Can it ever be that America, which has been raised only by Divine aid, will ever forget her God, lose sight of the obligations under which she rests, to advance the cause of Christianity, and thus bring wrath instead of blessing?"[13] With that, her school days were over.

Beginning with that visit on January 5, 1850, the courtship of Rutherford Hayes and Lucy Webb began in earnest. When he first called upon her that day, she did not - or perhaps *pretended* that she did not - remember him. He made sure she did not forget him again. With Uncle Birchard's financial help, he had moved his fledgling law practice to the larger city of Cincinnati, where he was in a position to frequently drop by the college for a visit. Lucy was now 18 years old and in her final year of college, and so into the age of marrying.

Rutherford was winnowing out the other girls, and winnowing in Lucy Webb. He very much liked this educated, cheerful young lady with the sunny disposition, who could sing, play the piano and guitar, and even do many bird whistles, but who also had a serious side of religious faith, compassion for her fellow humans, and a desire to end slavery. "Friend Jones has introduced me to more than one charming damsel; but still, for a country-bred boy, it's pleasanter to meet the natural gaiety of such an one as I fancy Miss Lucy must have become by this time, than any of the artificial attractions of your city belles," he wrote a friend. "P. S. Lest you should be troubled at not having mentioned Miss Lucy's whereabouts, I would simply say that I found her as soon as she returned from her holiday visit, and have enjoyed the light of her gleesome smile and merry talk times not a few nor far between."[14] It was not long before the couple were seriously in love.

In March of 1851 Lucy attended at least one of a series of lectures by John B. Gough, a 33-year-old former drunk who became a well known temperance advocate in the United States, Canada, and England. He had a reputation as a great speaker, and large crowds listened to his presentations. A great many people in Cincinnati attended and signed pledges to abstain from alcohol. "In his lectures

---

[13] "The Influence of Christianity on National Prosperity" by Lucy Webb, Papers.
[14] Diary, January 20, 1850.

he is especially severe upon the fashionable drinking of the day," Lucy wrote to her Aunt. "Several parties that I have attended lately have had the wine passing freely; to me there is no sight more sorrowful.... I have always been thankful that such strict temperance principles was taught to us."[15]

On June 22, 1851, Rutherford wrote a lengthy letter to Lucy telling of his love and feelings. "This love is, indeed, an awful thing," he wrote. "As Byron said, 'it interferes with all a man's projects for good and glory.' Besides, I am only fulfilling my scriptural destiny in 'forsaking father and mother' and all that... To think that that lovely vision is an actual, living, breathing being, and is loved by me, and loves in return, and will one day be my bride - my abiding, forgiving, trustful, loving wife - to make my happy home blessed indeed with her cheerful smile and silver voice and warm true heart!"[16]

Lucy felt the same way but did not let her letters get so carried away. "[T]here seems to be something providential about our acquaintance, its commencement, its renewal after a lapse of two or three years - and the happiness which is the result," Lucy wrote to Rutherford while on a trip to Columbus in August.[17] For a time Rutherford had a nickname for Lucy, "Gympsey."

In the summer of 1851 Lucy and Rutherford came to an agreement that they would be married. Because Rutherford felt he needed to get his law practice on a more firm footing in order to financially support a family, they had no specific date in mind and decided to keep the engagement a secret. Lucy gave him a ring which Rutherford wore the rest of his life.

This went on for more than a year, and finally they set a wedding day just before the end of 1852.

---

[15] Letter of Lucy to Aunt Marthesia, dated March 11, 1851.
[16] Diary, June 22, 1851.
[17] Letter of Lucy to Rutherford, August 20, 1851, Papers.

Chapter 3

THE EARLY YEARS TOGETHER

Lucy Webb did not marry a President of the United States, but rather a young man who never dreamed of being elected to the highest office in the land. When vows were exchanged on between 21-year-old Lucy Ware Webb and her 30-year-old beau, Rutherford Birchard Hayes, no one was speculating that this young couple would end up in the White House. He had never held political office and was working hard to establish a successful legal practice.

The wedding took place in Maria Webb's home in Cincinnati on the afternoon of December 30, 1852. Family and friends were in attendance, including Maria Webb, Sophia Hayes and Sardis Birchard, plus siblings, cousins and friends. The Reverend L. D. McCabe of Delaware, Ohio, a professor at Ohio Wesleyan University, was the minister who presided at the ceremony. Vows were exchanged, and the course for Lucy and Rutherford was set.

Life was off to a great start for the newlyweds. A few quotes from Rutherford's dairy proves his own state of bliss, and shows Lucy by reflection. Two months after the wedding Rutherford wrote that "[t]he great step of life which makes or mars the whole after journey, has been happily taken. The dear friend who is to share with me the joys and ills of our earthly being grows steadily nearer and dearer to me. A better wife I never hoped to have." He recorded that "[o]ur little differences in points of taste or preference are readily adjusted, and judging by the past I do not see how our tender and affectionate relations can be disturbed by any jar. She bears with my 'innocent peculiarities' so kindly, so lovingly; is so studious in providing for my little wants; is - is, in short, so true a wife that I cannot think it possible that any shadow of disappointment will ever cloud the prospect, save only such calamities as are the common allotment of Providence to all."

Without doubt he was enraptured with Lucy and with marriage. "Let me strive to be as true to her as she is to me. Let me too be loving, kind, and thoughtful." He felt his own shortcoming of expecting too much from others. "Especially," he wrote in self-reproach, "let me not permit the passion I have to see constant improvement in those I love, to be so blind in its eagerness as to wound a nature so tenderly sensitive as I know I sometimes have done." He closed his diary entry wondering, "Can anything enjoyed on earth be a source of truer, purer happiness - happiness more unalloyed than this? Blessings on his head who first invented marriage!"[1] Indeed, this was a young man in love. From everything we know, we can safely assume that Lucy felt the same way.

At the same time, Lucy and Rutherford were sharing the early days of his expanding legal practice. In January 1853, just nine days after the wedding, Rutherford wrote in his journal that he had that very day "the greatest triumph of my professional life, viz., arguing my first case orally in the Supreme Court of the state –'State of Ohio v. James Summons.'"[2] Then on April 11th he recorded that he "[a]rgued my first case in a court of the United States last week.... The case is one of great importance, viz., application to restrain the Junction Railroad Company from crossing Sandusky Bay on the ground, first, that it violates their charter, second, that it would obstruct the navigation of the bay."[3] Doubtless, Lucy shared the joy of Rutherford's triumphs as he moved into a full and successful practice.

Rutherford mused that same day reflected in his diary on what he was learning of the personality of Lucy. "My sweet wife is so diffident of her powers," he said concerning Lucy's lack of self-confidence. It was a problem that arose from time to time throughout her life. "I wish she could overcome it, so far at least as to make her willing to let me know precisely what she can and cannot do, so as never to feel the least hesitation in showing me the result of her efforts." There must have been some incident that he was thinking of, but the particulars were not recorded. "I love her better and better. She is infinitely superior in capacity to her own modest estimate of herself, and superior to most of those to whom she would look up. Come, love, never be ashamed of your work, when I am the sole judge."

The young couple were surely glad to see the financial independence which Rutherford was gaining for them in his law practice. In a letter to Uncle Birchard he proudly wrote that he "received more cash for fees the last month than any previous month in Cincinnati."[4]

---

[1] Diary, February 27, 1853.
[2] Diary, January 7, 1853.
[3] Diary, April 11, 1853.
[4] Diary, March 15, 1853.

Lucy was an abolitionist, and was proud of Rutherford when he took cases to defend runaway slaves who had come across the Ohio River from Kentucky. His handling of such cases may have led to an interesting event that happened on October 14, 1854. The family heard a cry from the German servant girl, named Anna, and when they came running they found she had discovered on the steps a box. Inside it was a naked black infant. They spent the evening and the next day working with a minister in getting the child into the Negro Orphans' Asylum of Cincinnati.[5]

In the winter of 1856 Rutherford had several runaway cases. The unusual cold that season froze the Ohio River to the point that people, and animals could walk across it from Covington, Kentucky, to freedom in Cincinnati, Ohio. Reportedly, thousands of black people that winter made their bid for a free life. Rutherford was shifting his own political attitude to join Lucy's abolitionism. When slave hunters tracked them down, lawsuits were filed to protect their new found liberty.

On March 14, 1853, the newlyweds posed before a camera. Photography was then still in its infancy, having been invented only fourteen years earlier by a Frenchman named Charles Daguerre. "Rutherford and I had our daguerreotypes taken," Lucy wrote. The light had to be perfect and the subject had to remain perfectly still for several seconds for the image to turn out properly on the copper plate steeped in chemicals. "No difficulty in getting pictures to suit us," she was able to say of the process. "The large one is for ourselves, that as old age draws on we might see what we once were." The enthusiasm of a new wife is evident. "Rutherford has that expression I love to see," she continued. "'Tis a mixed one, love, happiness, and a tinge of pride - enough to give a noble, manly air. And he seems to have just said, 'This is my wife.'"

Then she turned more reflective. "How dearly I will prize this picture. It will always bring sweet memories. And whatever shall be our lot, may he retain that look." She obviously spent a considerable time reflecting upon the images captured by the photographer that day, discussing them with her husband. Of Rutherford's look "I cannot tell all it shows. To me the greatest and best expression is only love." As for her own image, "I am pleased with mine. It has rather a meek, subdued air, clinging to its only support [i.e., Rutherford] - remove that and it will droop."

Other photographs were made in miniature and placed in a case as a gift for Aunt Lucy Cook. The young couple also studied those images. "Ruddy says mine is the best picture of me he ever saw. It has a little more independence than the others," she said, adding humourously, "at least, a stiffer head or neck. It may be a

---

[5] Diary, October 15, 1854.

prettier picture, but it does not show my heart so well. Dear Ruddy's darling face must be changed. It has the fierce look, so different from the first. Indeed I fear, when looking at it, he does not love me half so well; but that is only a daguerreotype story."

These words were written into Rutherford's diary by Lucy. At the conclusion, he took the book back and added: "What a dishonest artist he must be who can so misrepresent my features and expression as to give it a look which even seems to doubt between love and indifference towards you!"[6]

And so the months and early years passed. The early days of the marriage of Lucy Webb and Rutherford Hayes were spent in the same way as countless other young couples, then and now. They got know each other and learned to live together as a team. The young husband worked hard to establish himself professionally and financially, while the young wife devoted herself to managing the home and, soon enough, to raising a growing crop of children.

It was not long after the wedding that Lucy was expecting a baby. Rutherford hoped for, and believed he had a premonition that it would be, a boy. At two o'clock on the afternoon of Friday, November 6, 1853, "Lucy gave birth to their first child, a son. "How I love Lucy, the mother of my boy!" Rutherford wrote. In his new fatherhood he now saw Lucy in a new light. "Sweetheart and wife, she had been before, loved tenderly and strongly as such, but the new feeling is more 'home-felt,' quiet, substantial, and satisfying."

Of his feelings for the son, he wasn't sure how he felt on the very day of his birth. "For the 'lad' my feeling has yet to grow a great deal," he recorded honestly. "I prize him and rejoiced to have him, and when I take him in my arms begin to feel a father's love and interest, hope and pride, enough to know what the feeling will be if not what it is. I think what is to be his future, his life. How strange a mystery all this is! This to me is the beginning of a new life. A happy one, I believe. The mother and child are both 'resting' this quiet Sabbath morning. She on our bed, he on the lounge, and I alone with them, awake and musing...."[7]

On Christmas Day of 1853 the baby boy was christened Sardis Birchard Hayes. There is no doubt that in naming his son for his uncle Rutherford wanted to bestow upon Sardis Birchard a great honor. He wanted his uncle to know that he honored and loved him and appreciated all that he had done for him. The parents informed the extended family that the boy was to be called Cousin Birchard, or Birch, for short.[8] They soon called him "Birchie."

---

[6] Diary, March 16, 1853.
[7] Diary, November 8, 1853.
[8] Diary, December 25, 1853.

Rutherford's law practice was becoming very successful, taking him around the state on numerous business trips. This has benefitted us today because Lucy would often write to him while he was away, and these letters have been preserved. The record of correspondence provides us with an insight into to them and their relationship we would not otherwise have. Writing on April 15, 1854, to "Dear Ruddy," Lucy wrote concerning their five month old son. "I am very well and have the milk he wants, which is one great cause for his good behavior," she said. "He is no trouble at night and very little (if any) during the day." Her mothering instincts were at high tide at this time in her life. "Oh what an inestimable treasure he is. How the heart is drawn towards him, and all happiness centered in our darling. The more I love him the dearer is my dearest Ruddy to me."[9]

This letter illustrates two of the themes of the life of Lucy Hayes. First, she was above all else an individual who found her greatest fulfillment in her family life. She was not in the least unwilling in this regard; being a wife and raising her children was always a central theme and joy in her life. It was never a burden to her, or something to be resented as an imposition on her own personal time. She always sought to do good in the outside world, but only within this greater context. Years later when she became the First Lady of the United States, she placed that experience as only a sub-text of her family role. Both as a young mother and as a middle aged woman, she gladly lived her life as a woman of the nineteenth century, and within the traditions of that day.

A second great truth revealed in this same letter is that she loved people, and cultivated and treasured relationships with family and friends. "I am very happy with Sister Fanny and Mother - everything so pleasant and every one so kind," she wrote. She mentioned a few of the many people who were within the circle of her life. "Callie and her two little ones spent the day here last Thursday. They are very sweet and interesting, especially little Carrie. Mrs. Cami L. is as dear to me as ever. No one could help loving and esteeming her who knew her as I do." She went to also mention Miss Woods, brother Jim, and Mr. and Mrs. Orr.[10] Rutherford felt the same way about people. Family and friends were always an important part of her, and their, happiness.

Three weeks later Rutherford was still gone, and she wrote again. It is true that the letters and writings of that era were, to our eyes today, overly romanticized and sentimental, but this is no reason to discount the sincerity of the writer's feelings. "You, dearest," Lucy wrote, "are ever in my thoughts." She

---

[9] Letter Lucy to Rutherford, April 15, 1854, Papers.
[10] Ibid.

went on to explain that young Birchie was up early that Saturday morning "when the bright sun was pouring the light in upon us. Oh, no, he must be up, and then I took him in my arms [and] what a beautiful smile rewarded me."[11]

This and many other letters of Lucy also reveal another of her traits, that she was very much affected throughout her life by the weather. She drew strength from the sun, its light and warmth making her feel light and warm inwardly. "Today is beautiful," she wrote once in a typical statement, "the sun so clear and bright, that I am compelled to feel bright myself."[12] On the other hand, rain, clouds and snow made her feel downcast. She would write such things as, "[a] rainy dreary Sunday afternoon with no dear husband to chase away sad thoughts,"[13] and "[a] gloomy rainy day".[14] "The rain has poured incessantly." she wrote her husband and brother while they were gone during the Civil War. "How often we think of you all when the rain is pouring down, and wonder whether our dear ones are marching."[15]

Throughout her life as a mother Lucy Hayes had the good fortune of always having domestic help in the form of servants for the home and sometimes what were called "nurses" for the children. Even before she had any children they had servants, and she complained to her sister that having three servants in so small a family was too much. This was by no means the typical experience of American parents of the 1850s. The Hayes family, however, was a wealthy one, from the huge wealth of Uncle Birchard and increasingly from Rutherford's successful law practice. It has been said that by the time he reached the White House Rutherford was the richest of all Presidents who served during the 1800s.

Daily assistance in the house was a blessing they were always to enjoy. In a letter to Uncle Sardis, who was often called Uncle Birchard, Rutherford wrote that "Lucy and her mother have gone to church. I am staying at home to see that Birchard and his nurse get into no trouble. The little fellow has just got over his first cold."[16] Lucy commented once that the Sabbath, for her, was a day of more work than usual rather than rest. She felt the servants should have that day off from work, so Lucy ended up with the care of the children each Sunday.[17]

In 1855 Lucy described her daily life in a letter to her mother-in-law, Sophia Hayes. "Our household affairs move on in the same routine," she said, "cooking, washing, baking, house cleaning, watching Birchie, making some clothes and

[11] Letter Lucy to Rutherford, May 6, 1854, Papers.
[12] Letter Lucy to Rutherford, October 1861, Papers.
[13] Letter Lucy to Rutherford, March 2, 1862, Papers.
[14] Letter Lucy to Rutherford, March 21, 1862, Papers.
[15] Letter Lucy to Rutherford, April 22, 1862, Papers.
[16] Diary, March 5, 1854.
[17] Letter Lucy to Rutherford, March 2, 1862, Papers.

altering last summer's dresses." She then goes on to mention her domestic help situation. "Annie leaves us tomorrow. Her successor is now with us, a large good natured looking damsel."[18]

With a young child in tow, Rutherford and Lucy were looking to move into a new and large home. They found a home they liked and looked to Uncle Birchard for help.[19] Ever the loving father, and the possessor of a fortune which delighted in using to help his only nephew, the bachelor uncle came through for the young couple. The money for the house was sent late in September. The price was $4,500, plus another thousand spent on improvements and furnishings. Rutherford and Lucy were appreciative and dutifully and excitedly reported to him of their experiences.

Throughout August Ruddy wisely worked at fixing it up so that it was all ready before they moved in.[20] The happy day of moving came on September 4, 1854, and was duly recorded in the diary. "Moved, or began to move, to my new home, my own house (if the sale is confirmed), No. 383 Sixth Street; south side, west of Mound. A muss it is to move; all sorts of laughing over our loads of furniture, a good deal of it Lucy's mother's when she went to housekeeping - good, but old; a great sending of it back and forth for cleaning, varnishing, making as good as new; but finally all settled comfortably, pleasantly. First meal in the house, spoons, knives, and forks forgotten! All use a little silver knife and fork presented to Birchie by his uncle William Hayes, and an old spoon picked up by Birchie for a plaything."

One of their first priorities in the new house was to set up a room for Uncle Birchard to come and stay. "We are not entirely through 'putting to rights' yet," Rutherford wrote proudly to his Uncle, "but have got your room in order; so you can come down any day. When you get to the Hamilton depot take your carpetbag in hand, the walk is short, save your quarter, and keep along the south side of Sixth Street till you get to No. 383, next house east of Glenn's. My name is on the door, walk straight in and the third-story front chamber is ready for you."[21]

Raising young Birchie was the main activity and a great joy for Lucy. His father reported that he was "[a] large fine boy, bright blue or dark gray eyes; fine, intelligent, and mild as summer; sandy hair, fair complexion, a lovely laughing face; always in motion, fond of sport, excellent disposition--and we love him so

---

[18] Letter L to Sophia Hayes, 1855, Papers.
[19] Diary, July 23, 1854.
[20] Diary, August 1 and September 4, 1854.
[21] Diary, September 17, 1854.

much. We are as happy as [a] heart could wish." Thinking of Lucy, he wrote, "His mother improves in all things, and is so tender and thoughtful in all things.[22]

During the 1850s Lucy and Rutherford closely followed what was going on in the increasingly turbulent political world. They were confirmed Whigs, and Rutherford had cast his first vote for Henry Clay for President in 1844. They also supported, and he voted for, the Whig candidates in 1848, Zachary Taylor, and in 1852, Winfield Scott. They were disappointed when the Southern dominated Democratic Party won the presidency with Franklin Pierce. When the Whig Party thereafter disintegrated, Lucy liked the newly forming anti-slavery Republicans, and convinced Rutherford to join them. Like all women of the day, of course, Lucy could not vote. Rutherford always kept his hand in local politics, and closely watched events nationally as the slave crisis worsened throughout the decade of the 1850s. In 1856 they supported the Republican presidential candidate, John C. Fremont, who lost to Democrat James Buchanan.

The winter of 1854-1855 was a cold one, but the hearth and hearts of the Hayes family were warm and glowing. " It is the coldest day of the year. The freezing northwest wind is sweeping through the street," Rutherford wrote to a friend in January. "Here I sit in my cozy little parlor, my wife Lucy sewing almost within kissing distance, my table covered with law papers. Overhead I can hear the two grandmothers--Grandmothers Hayes and Webb--talking and answering 'the boy' (as if there was no other boy!) while he seems to be hammering the floor with a mallet--it may be the heel of one of my boots."[23] This entry reflects happy home, indeed.

At 5:30 p.m. on Thursday, March 20, 1856, Lucy gave birth to a second child. He was named Webb Cook Hayes in honor of Lucy's family name. Although the birth was expected, when the time actually came Rutherford could not find a doctor to handle the situation. Three doctors were out, but at last Lucy's brother, Dr. Joseph Webb, arrived to help his sister. No longer being of service, Rutherford in the tradition of earlier days sat down in another room and waited, keeping himself entertained by reading the papers of Thomas Jefferson.[24]

Through the coming months Lucy spent her time with the newborn, whom she called (for a while) "Samson,"[25] and Birchie, still just two years old. Any mother in that situation was fortunate to have servants helping.

The summer of 1856 was a sad one for the Hayes family. Rutherford was extremely close to his sister, Fanny Hayes Platt, who became deathly ill in giving

---

[22] Diary, October 4, 1854.
[23] Diary, January 22, 1855.
[24] Diary, March 23, 1856.
[25] Diary, June 10, 1856.

birth to twins in June. The infants both died. It had been a difficult pregnancy and a most physically distressing birth, more than Fanny's body could withstand. The family was alarmed and relieved as Fanny's health alternately sank and recovered. Rutherford wrote that he would like to go to quietly into her house and sit, without her even knowing if his mother felt that his presence would distress Fanny.[26]

Rutherford and Fanny had been very close, closer than most brothers and sisters. Lucy, too, had grown to love Fanny. When she was near death, Fanny spoke of Lucy. "Once when she supposed she was dying we all gathered around her and brought in her children," Rutherford wrote later. "She spoke a few kind words to all and spoke of the absent. Turning to me, with her sweetest smile, those beautiful blue eyes, she said: 'Oh, dear Lucy and the boys, how I wish I could see them again but I never shall'; and again: 'Dear Lucy and the boys, how I wish I had talked more about them.'" Rutherford brought in little Ruddy, Fanny's child and his namesake. "When I brought in little Ruddy, she put her hands lovingly on his pretty fat arms, shoulders, and cheeks, saying: 'Dear boy - sweet child,' and smiled oh, so lovingly. I held one of her hands rubbing it gently. Little Ruddy observing it took the other and rubbed it smiling happily. Fanny said: 'I am going this time.' Little Ruddy spoke up: 'Where are you going, mother?' She replied: 'To Heaven, up to Heaven, I hope, where we shall soon all meet again.'

When Fanny died on July 16, 1856, Rutherford was immeasurably distressed.[27] Lucy, of course, shared in the loss of Fanny. Rutherford had lost a sister; she had lost a friend.

In the summer of 1857 the travel tables turned, and Lucy went on a trip to the Cook family home in Chillicothe, leaving Rutherford behind in Cincinnati. The trip was fatiguing and took is toll on her physically. "When we reached Aunt M's I could hardly walk, my back felt as though it would certainly give way, and my head was in the same condition." Headaches, unfortunately, became a common theme for the remainder of her life. She would frequently mention in letters such things as "I intended to have written a long letter...but have had...[a] sick headache for the last week,[28]" and "I have been having [a] sick headache so much."[29]

Rutherford Platt Hayes was born on June 24, 1858 in Cincinnati, in the same room where Webb made his first appearance. The "Platt" was after the family

---

[26] Diary, June 28, 1856.
[27] Diary, July 1856.
[28] Letter Lucy to Rutherford, dated 1863, Papers.
[29] Letter Lucy to Rutherford, dated May 3, 1863, Papers.

name of his deceased sister, Fanny Hayes Platt. Lucy did well for about two weeks after the birth, but then came down with a severe cold. "She had severe pains in her breasts; and for ten days has had rheumatism creeping over her from one place to another, giving her great pain," wrote Rutherford. "It began in her left shoulder and arm and in her neck and having passed almost over her is now, we think, leaving her."[30]

Over the years the Hayes family came to love the Christmas season, and they seem to have celebrated it in ways surprisingly like today. Based on her known later love for the holiday, there is every reason to believe that Lucy felt the same way about Christmas as was expressed by Rutherford in his letters and diary. "Merry Christmas to you, dear Fanny!" he wrote in am 1853 letter to his sister on the first Christmas Day after his marriage to Lucy.[31] In his dairy a year later he inscribed, "A merry Christmas."[32] He reported to his uncle in 1855 that he gave Birchie a little chair for Christmas,[33] and in 1856 wished his uncle "Merry Christmas and a happy New Year to all!"[34] In his diary entry that year Rutherford wrote, "What a triumphant day for him [Birchie] Christmas was! He found in his stockings a picture-book and knicknacks."[35]

"Merry Christmas 1857," Rutherford recorded on December 25th. "Birchie's first genuine Christmas. How he talked of 'Old Chris Kringle.' Hanging up stockings, springing up in bed to see if Chris heard when I blew a tin trumpet. And how happy he was when he got up and saw his drum and table and toys and candy."[36]

It was even better the next year. "Our children are overflowing with enjoyment of their Christmas presents. It is a great happiness to observe them," Rutherford recorded. "Last evening we had a jolly time. Our German [servant] girls, without our suspecting it, worked night before last until three o'clock in the morning in the cellar, and succeeded in surprising us all when we went to supper last evening, by giving us a beautiful Christmas tree. Birch and Webb were hardly able to contain themselves.... This morning they are again in a happy excitement over the leavings of 'Kriss Kringle.' I do not think I ever enjoyed a Christmas so much when I was a little fellow, as I do now in seeing the happiness of my

---

[30] Diary, July 23, 1858.
[31] Diary, December 25, 1853.
[32] Diary, December 25, 1854.
[33] Diary, December 26, 1855.
[34] Diary, December 28, 1856.
[35] Ibid.
[36] Diary, December 25, 1857.

children."[37] Christmas greetings, stockings, trees, "Chris Kringle" and gifts are certainly all very familiar holiday items today.

Lucy was on a trip to see her family for the Christmas of 1860, leaving her husband in Cincinnati. On Christmas Eve Rutherford was at home, lonely, writing in his dairy. "Christmas eve. Lucy gone to Chillicothe.... All ought to be at home to make home happy on these festal days. Boys well; hardly know what they want 'Old Chris' to bring them."[38] Had Lucy known that her husband would himself be gone to war for the next four Christmases, she would have stayed home that year.

Religion and the life of church-going Christians were woven soul-deep into Rutherford and Lucy Hayes. It was a part of them, and a part of their lives. "We have just returned from church," Lucy wrote to her mother in March of 1855. "Our minister has been delivering a course of lectures on home which were very interesting. We are all much pleased with him."[39] In another letter Lucy mentioned in an off-handed way in a letter than "when the Spirit moves I always obey."[40]

Yet inwardly she sometimes struggled with her Christian ideal and her actual performance in life. "If my life was that of the faithful Christian - my idea of a true love of our dear Savior," she once wrote, "I would feel that all was well, but why I do not live as I always wish, and yet hope to, is one of the strange things of life."[41] This, of course, is the dilemma of all people who wish to live a certain standard, and finding that they do not always do so.

She mentioned this issue again years later during the Civil War. "This morning I went to hear Rev. Mr. Trimble preach - taking Birch and little Rud with me - the sermon was very good- the little boys behaved so well- that I felt quite happy," she wrote to Rutherford. "[B]ut then when all is pleasant and happy around me, the desire is with me so earnest and anxious, that I was only a true Christian. I try to read my Bible and pray for the safety of those dear to me but of myself all is rain and cold. What would I not give to feel and view things as Mrs. Dr. Davis. To her the future is all peace and joy. I can never talk to any one of these things - not even to you - and so I grope along at times trying so earnestly, then again indifferent. I almost despair of ever being what I so earnestly desire."[42]

The issue persisted throughout Lucy's life. "One thing troubles me - I am not the sincere earnest Christian woman that I am represented to be," she wrote in 1880 when she was First Lady and accused in the press of being "too" Christian.

---

[37] Diary, December 26, 1858.
[38] Diary, December 24, 1860.
[39] Letter Lucy to Maria Webb, dated March 1855, Papers.
[40] Letter Lucy to Laura, dated April 6, 1862, Papers.
[41] Letter Lucy to Rutherford, dated June 4, 1862, Papers.
[42] Letter Lucy to Rutherford, dated August 30, 1863, Papers.

"[H]ow humble and unworthy I feel. And then I feel they [confused] me with my dear Mother. The words suit her, but not the daughter."[43]

Rutherford was always less committed than Lucy, though religion was always something important to him. Neither he nor Lucy were followers of a particular denomination, though they generally went to Methodist Church throughout their married life. He had been baptized as and infant and raised in the Presbyterian church, then attended Episcopalian services at college, but after marrying attended Methodist services with Lucy. "I am not a subscriber to any creed. I belong to no church," he wrote many years later. "But in a sense, satisfactory to myself and believed by me to be important, I try to be a Christian, or rather I want to be a Christian and to help do Christian work."[44] This they both did. They read the Bible, tried to live by its precepts, observed the Sabbath, attended church services regularly, prayed daily, raised their children in their faith, and did all that was within their power to lead a Christian life. They knew they were not perfect, but they also knew that they were truly doing the best they could.

On June 8, 1859, Birchard, Webb and young Rutherford were baptized in the parlor of their own home by Dr. Clark of the Methodist Church. Both grandmothers were present for the occasion, along with their Uncle James Webb, the servants and the parents. When it was over, three year old Webb asked, "What did the gentleman put water on my head for?"[45]

The young boys were taking note of their religious environment. "Birch and Webb often discuss deep questions touching God, death, a future state, and the like. Birch is reverent and orthodox in his views; Webb is inquiring and by no means as serious as would seem proper," Rutherford mused in his diary. "The other day in a thunderstorm they fell into a conversation on the cause of lightning. Birch said God did it. Webb interrupted, "Does God make the elephants?" 'Yes, Webby.'- 'Well, how does he get them down?' puts in Webb. 'Oh,' says Birch, 'there are a great many things about God that we can't understand.' - 'Well, but,' said Webb, 'who made God?' 'Webby,' said Birch very seriously, 'that is one of the things we can't understand. We shall know about that when we die and go to Heaven.'"[46]

In 1858 Rutherford held political officer for the first time. In December he was appointed by the Cincinnati City Council as the city attorney, called the City Solicitor. His predecessor had been killed in an accident, and after a close vote of the Councilmen he filled out the remainder of the term. The position carried with

---

[43] Letter Lucy to "friend," dated June 1880, Papers.
[44] Diary, May 17, 1890.
[45] Diary, June 19, 1859.
[46] Diary, April 11, 1860.

it a salary of $3,500, which was sufficient to support his family and became his primary income. In April of 1859 he was elected to a term of his own, the first rung on a ladder that would reach all the way to the presidency.

Life was in full bloom for the Hayes. With three children, Lucy was busier than ever with family matters. They spent the last half of the summer out of their home while a third story was put on the back part of the house, which provided a brick kitchen, wash room, servant's room and a bathroom. Always interested in new inventions, they installed a kitchen range and other conveniences. "I never enjoyed life better." Rutherford wrote to Uncle Birchard. "Barring two or three anxious weeks on the boys' accounts, this has been a happy winter-- very. Lucy is in finer feather than she has been for two or three years."[47]

Then came the Civil War, and everything changed.

---

[47] Diary, February 4, 1860.

Chapter 4

THE CIVIL WAR

The Civil War had been a long time coming, and when it burst forth in April of 1861 it was not really a surprise to anyone. Slavery had been dividing Americans since the Declaration of Independence, and it proved to be an issue incapable of solution. The generation of Rutherford and Lucy Hayes was the one destined to deal with this great struggle.

In the 1860 presidential election Lucy supported, and Rutherford voted for, Republican presidential candidate Abraham Lincoln. He ran on a promise that he would not disturb slavery where it was, but he would allow it to go no further. Southern radicals promised that if he won, they would secede from the Union. Lincoln won without any support at all from any Southern state, and in response some Southern states did pull out of the Union. Perhaps Lucy agreed with Rutherford, who thought that perhaps the experiment of uniting free and slave states into one nation was a failure, and to let the slave states go out of the Union.[1]

President-elect Lincoln of Illinois had to travel to Washington to be inaugurated, and his route took him through Cincinnati. Lucy and Rutherford went to Indianapolis and rode the presidential train with him to their home town. They witnessed Lincoln ride in an open carriage, standing erect with his hat off, bowing to the cheering crowds. Rutherford appreciated the simplicity of the procession, feeling that the fancy horses and carriages in those troubled times would have detracted from the scene. He was favorably impressed with the man, and so probably was Lucy.[2]

The new President was inaugurated on March 4, 1861, amid an unprecedented national crisis. Unlike Rutherford, he felt that he said taken an oath

---

[1] Dairy January 27, 1861.
[2] Diary, February 15, 1861.

to preserve and protect the Constitution of the United States, and that he could not let the Southern states go. Meanwhile, a new government calling itself the Confederate States of America was formed in Montgomery, Alabama.

In this excited situation, Rutherford became a very early political casualty of the war. The Democrats and Know-Nothings of Cincinnati fused together and charged that the Republicans were unable to handle the crisis, and in the local election on April 1, 1861, Rutherford was defeated for re-election as City Solicitor. Out of his primary job and income, he had to go back to a private law practice to support Lucy and the boys. Fortunately, he was able to take over the practice of another lawyer who Lincoln had just appointed as minister to Ecuador.[3]

On April 12, 1861, the shooting started when the Confederate forces surrounding Fort Sumter in Charleston, South Carolina, opened fire on United States forces. The fort's defenders were compelled to surrender, resulting in a great indignation throughout the Northern states. Rutherford and Lucy were no longer content to let the South go. "We are all for war," he wrote to Uncle Birchard. "A great change for two weeks to produce.... Lucy enjoys it and wishes she had been in Fort Sumter with a garrison of women."[4] President Lincoln called for volunteers from across America to raise troops to put down the rebellion.

War, then, was what Rutherford and Lucy Hayes would get. It didn't have to be that way, but was so because they were voluntary participants in it. When the deadly strife began, Rutherford could have sat it all out. As a young man he had stayed out of the Mexican War because he, like many Northern Whigs, felt it was an immoral war fought to steal land from Mexico for the expansion of Southern slave territory. This time, however, things were very different. At 38 years of age, he was old enough to say that he was too old, and lacking in military training, to serve. Few would have criticized such a position. There was no draft law in 1861 compelling him to go. But sitting it out was not his way or his wish. Instead of leaving the burden to others, once it was clear that the war was for real and there would be no political solution, Rutherford plunged into the fray. When Governor William Dennison offered him the position of major in a new regiment designated as the 23rd Ohio Volunteers, Rutherford accepted.[5]

Lucy was in complete support of this. She wrote that "the Northern heart" was fired, that "the enthusiasm that prevails in our city is perfectly irresistible" [sic], and that "what will be our next duty we cannot tell."[6] Inwardly, of course,

---

[3] Geer, pp. 44-45.
[4] Diary, April 15, 1861.
[5] Diary June 7, 1861.
[6] Letter by Lucy Hayes, dated April 15, 1861, Papers.

she felt the inevitable worries of a wife for her husband's absence and safety, but she wanted above all to be a good soldier's wife. Adding to the emotional mix of those days and feelings was the fact that she was pregnant once again, due by the end of the year.

Rutherford was immediately put into the field for the training of his regiment in a race track in Columbus. At ten o'clock on the night of June 10th he shot off a quick note to Lucy. "You know how I love you; how I love the family all," he said, still trying to explain himself, "but Lucy, I am much happier in this business than I could be fretting away in the old office near the court house. It is living. My only regret is that you don't like our location. We shall probably spend the summer here, or a good part of it, unless we go into Virginia. No more tonight. Much love."[7] Realizing that their letters would be a great treasure one day, Rutherford told Lucy to "keep all these scrawls for future reference."[8]

The frequent letters between Lucy and Rutherford tell a great and wonderful story, giving voice in the present tense to the life they lived at the time. The letters are expressed so well that they bear frequent quotation to give an understanding of Lucy's heart and experiences. There is no need for the historian to interfere with a paraphrase where a historical figure can tell the story so well by herself.

Deep emotions of patriotism for her country, enthusiasm for a cause she supported, love for husband, and fear for what may be ahead, gripped Lucy as her husband departed. Her letters are steeped in these sentiments. "My greatest happiness now would be to fee that I was doing something for the comfort and happiness of our men," she wrote Rutherford in June 1861. "I feel that in giving you up (for dearest it is hard to feel we may be parted) I have tried to do cheerfully and without murmur what was my duty." She hoped that "you will find, Ruddy, that your foolish little trial of a wife was fit to be a soldier's wife."[9] Lucy was able to take Birchie and visit Rutherford at his camp near Columbus, called Camp Chase.

Lucy was pleased that her brother, Dr. Joseph Webb, was appointed as the surgeon in Rutherford's regiment, and that the two would serve together in what was to come. Sophia Hayes, a frequent nay sayer, wondered why any man with a happy home would want to leave it, which offended Lucy. On the morning of July 25, 1861, Lucy tearfully bade her husband and brother goodbye as they departed for western Virginia.[10] They knew not whether they would ever see each other again.

---

[7] Diary, June 10, 1861.
[8] Diary, July 27, 1861.
[9] Letter Lucy to Rutherford, dated June 13, 1861, Papers.
[10] Geer, pp. 46-47.

The Hayes boys, young though they were, in their own childish ways knew that there was a war, that their father was gone to it, and that he was in harm's way. "Birchie says tell Papa that I prayed for him and asked God to take care of him," Lucy wrote Rutherford. "Webb says ask him if he wants me and Birch up there."[11]

Sitting at home, hearing of the war and its ceaseless and tormenting rumors, put Lucy into a constant condition of anxiety about the well being of her husband. "Dear Rutherford," she wrote, "I picked up the paper this morning, and...there I saw the appointments of Surgeons. I can't help I have cried myself almost sick.... I have kept down my feelings. I have almost smothered myself trying to appear cheerful and willing to let you go... but it is all useless for me to cry and be so unhappy for I fear you will be angry with me for my feelings." It was a day of difficult emotions for Lucy, and her old lack of self-confidence crept back into her mind. "I always feel that you lack a little confidence in me, and think that when I tell you how wretchedly I feel that I have been talking myself into it. Let me assure you nobody but yourself has every heard me say anything about this business."[12]

The weeks passed by and Lucy slowly became somewhat more accustomed to her new role. "We are always so glad to receive your letters," she wrote on August 9th. "They cannot come too often, but with me I have nothing to write except assurances of my love - my hopes and fears. No, I do not let myself have fears - so far I have kept a bright future before me."[13] Of course, she and Rutherford did have a very bright future ahead of them, but they did not know the end from the beginning. She reported on the boys and the extended family she was then visiting.

On September 5th Lucy wrote that "I begin to realize more and more your absence. I find myself listening for your voice, then I think of how many weeks perhaps months may pass without seeing you." She turned to her own situation at home. With Rutherford's cut in salary from successful attorney to military officer, Lucy was on a reduced income. "I suppose we will have very hard times, and I want to live as carefully and economically as I can," she wrote.[14] A few months later she reported that "I am getting to be quite a business woman."[15]

In the middle of September came a letter from Rutherford, telling of his first experience in combat. Here was the dreaded event, her husband facing death.

[11] Ibid.
[12] Letter Lucy to Rutherford, dated July 1, 1861, Papers.
[13] Letter Lucy to Rutherford, dated August 9, 1861, Papers.
[14] Letter Lucy to Rutherford, dated September 5, 1861, Papers.
[15] Letter Lucy to Rutherford, dated April 23, 1862, Papers.

"Well, darling, we have had our first battle," he wrote. "You have often heard of the feelings of men in the interval between the order of battle and the attack. Matthews, myself, and others were rather jocose in our talk, and my actual feeling was very similar to what I have when going into an important trial--not different nor more intense. I thought of you and the boys and the other loved ones, but there was no such painful feeling as is sometimes described."[16] That the feelings of dread before a battle and before a trial are similar would be no surprise to any attorney.

The political situation in the country was something that Lucy kept herself informed about. After all, national news was now personal news for the safety of her husband and the future of her family hung in the balance. The early days of the Civil War did not go well for the North, with military setbacks and apparent political indecision. Lucy lost her patience with the new President. "At times we have such conflicting rumors of troubles in the Cabinet, then the present trouble of Gen. Fremont, till I feel almost crazed and think there are no true men among our leaders," she wrote in exasperation to Rutherford on September 23rd. "President Lincoln, I fear, lacks decision - he is too easy."[17] The next month she asked her husband, "Do you ever feel [as] mad as a March Hare with all the Generals and most especially with the President of these United States?"

In many respects the life of the people of Cincinnati went on as usual, war or no war. Baby Ruddy became very sick in late September and fears of his death arose, but fortunately he turned the corner and recovered. A minister sent to the local congregation was found unacceptable by the people, something which Lucy found to be a difficult subject. The city of Cincinnati was divided into sewing circles to make warm clothing for the soldiers.

Lucy, as she always did, took renewed strength from good weather. "Today is beautiful," she wrote in October, "the sun so clear and bright, that I am compelled to feel bright myself." Birch had a birthday. Uncle Birchard sent crates of apples from his home called Spiegel Grove in Fremont, Ohio, to Lucy and the boys, a commodity which was scarce and expensive in Cincinnati. Lucy told him how much gladness the supply of apples was to them over the weeks. To Rutherford, however, she wrote of her insecurity. "Uncle Birchard with his usual kindness has sent me apples," she said. "I often wonder whether he really can like me or only tolerates for your sake, any way he writes me very kind letters."

Rutherford commented on the people back home in a letter dated October 19, 1861. "No, Lucy, the newspapers mislead you," he said, apparently in reference to

---

[16] Diary, September 11, 1861.
[17] Letter Lucy to Rutherford, dated September 23, 1861, Papers.

articles on the sufferings of the soldiers in the field. " It is the poor families at home, not the soldiers, who can justly claim sympathy.... I feel for the poor women and children in Cincinnati. The men out here have sufferings, but no more than men of sense expected, and were prepared for, and can bear."[18]

It was not long before there arose a great controversy about what the Union Army ought to do with runaway slaves, called "contraband," who fled to freedom behind the Northern lines within the slave states. This early in the war it was not the goal of the President or of the Congress to free the slaves, and many white people, including Union generals, thought they ought to be sent back South. Lucy did not agree. "Above all things, Ruddy," she wrote emphatically in October, "if a contraband is in Camp - don't let the 23rd Regiment be disgraced by returning [him] or anything of the kind." She concluded by saying, "do not think I am proving myself unfit for a soldier's wife - a smiling face is generally seen but the heartache is concealed."[19]

Physical reminders of absent loved ones touched the hearts of those at home. Lucy's brother, Dr. Joseph Webb, had his horse was sent home from the field. When his mother and Lucy saw it, it affected them so much that "to tell the truth, mother and I both cried a wee bit."[20] Simple physical things that had just come from the presence of loved ones took on a new and deep meaning. A month later a trunk was sent back to Cincinnati. "When...we opened it, and so many of your and brother Joe's clothes," Lucy wrote to Rutherford, "it was a very sad feeling. We had heard rumors of battle or expected battle... I could hardly retain my self command, but tried to look at the bright side, and now I am in constant hope of happy days."[21] She was a trooper, always telling herself of the good to crowd out thoughts of the bad.

In his diary, which he steadily kept in the field as well as at home, Rutherford made an entry on Monday, December 23, 1861. "Wet, cold, windy; sleet last night. At dinner today with Captain Sperry and Lieutenant Kennedy, I was handed the following dispatch: 'Cincinnati, December 23, 1861. Lieutenant-Colonel R. B. Hayes, Twenty-third Regiment. Wife and boy doing well. Stranger arrived Saturday evening, nine o'clock p. m. J. T. Webb.'" His fourth son had been born.

"I preferred a daughter," the father honestly confided to his diary, "but in these times when women suffer so much, I am not sure but we ought to rejoice that our girls are boys. What shall I call him? What will Birch say, and Webb, and Babes [i.e., Rud]? 'Babes' no longer. He is supplanted by the little stranger. Cold

---

[18] Diary, October 19, 1861.
[19] Letter Lucy to Rutherford, dated October 1861, Papers.
[20] Ibid.
[21] Letter Lucy to Rutherford, dated November 1861, Papers.

wind and snow-storm outside. Dear Lucy! I hope she will keep up good heart." He sent a telegraph back home: "Congratulations and much love to mother and son. All well."[22]

Christmas of 1861 was spent with Lucy recovering from delivering the new boy, and Rutherford in the field. Lucy started the new year of 1862 with a letter reporting on the new family member. "Our little fourth boy was two weeks old last night." She reported that she had been "very careful" about her own recovery from the birth, and that "today for the first time left my bed." She wanted to get Rutherford's agreement to name him Joseph. "Our little boy - or little Joseph as the children call him and I wish - is a nice baby, not very large, a plump face, a mouth like brother Joe's, nose like Webb's, and dark blue eyes... He now has the colic."[23]

Rutherford agreed - the name would be Joseph, after Lucy's brother. He would prove to be a severe trial to her, being constantly with the colic. In March the problems continued. "Little Joseph is growing very little, but he is a pretty and sweet baby. Uncle Joe will yet be proud of him." Lucy wrote. "I feel disheartened about the poor little fellow ever getting over the colic. It is painful to me to witness his sufferings. Mother agrees with me that it is different from the other children. He notices a great deal, and will be happy when he has a moment free from pain."[24]

Eight days later things had not improved. "It is getting late, but all day our poor little Joe has cried and worried so that I have had no time to anything but trot-trot and tap and try all ways of holding him but nothing can ease the colic," Lucy reported. "He is now at nine o'clock asleep with his grandmother, or rather, they are in the large rocking chair, both asleep."[25]

Lucy always had a difficult relationship with her mother in law, Sophia Birchard Hayes. During 1862 she was invited to Fremont to Uncle Birchard's home at Spiegel Grove for an extended stay. When she learned that Sophia was to be there, too, Lucy cringed. The mother was too negative, and wore on Lucy's happy spirit. She wrote to Rutherford that "I several times thought I would try and ask you whether Mother Hayes would be one of our family at Fremont - but I could not do it." She then went on to discuss the difficult situation of the poor relationship, trying to express her true feelings without offending Rutherford by criticizing his mother. "I feel, R, that I would be sure to have some unhappy ending" if Sophia was there.

---

[22] Diary, December 23, 1861.
[23] Letter Lucy to Rutherford, dated January 5, 1862, Papers.
[24] Letter Lucy to Rutherford, dated March 2, 1862, Papers.
[25] Letter Lucy to Rutherford, dated March 13, 1862, Papers.

After confessing that "I know very well my own weakness," she went on to get to the main point. "Mother H is peculiar and does not, nor can she, regard me with much love. I cannot tell you why I know it, but I feel it beyond all doubt." She went on to explain that Uncle Birchard was already sick and unused to small children being around, and to add Mother Hayes who has "such different ideas of governing children" would just be too much for him.

Lucy worried about how Rutherford would answer her letter. "Oh Ruddy can you not see why I am fearful... When you answer this, dear R., do not write hastily to me, do not let this which is the hardest thing I ever did cause you to say one cold word."[26] It turned out Lucy was overly worried about the situation. Rutherford had never been particularly close to his mother, and was well aware that she was often strict, humorless, negative and tactless. He supported his wife's feelings and wishes, and the entire plan of having the extended family live together was indefinitely postponed.

As was part of life before the twentieth century, illness and the menace of death from disease was ever-present. "Our little Ruddy has been very sick all fall - chills and fever - and with the chills a tendency to spasms," Lucy informed her husband. "We thought at one time he would not live, the spasms were very severe. Then I was very unwell myself, was not able to do anything for some time, and a constant stab of anxiety about Ruddy."[27]

Baby Joseph also continued to suffer. "Yesterday was more gloomy to me than usual. I could not shake off the feeling of depression. Our little Joe, all morning fretted and cried, and I could not help thinking of almost three months passed and still no prospect of the deal little fellow getting over it." Three days later she wrote "the more trouble I suppose the more love."[28]

Lucy wrote that the day was "a bright beautiful day - the children well and happy - little Joe improving - everything to make life pleasant and joyous but the absence of the one who is dearer than anything else. I think of you constantly...if I could only know what you were doing, where you were. But the uncertainty oh it is dreadful.... The dread feeling is with me that you are even now marching. We are not separated, for I feel that you constantly think of me with so much love." She also reported that the famous little Tom Thumb was in town. Young Ruddy and Webb went to see him. Birch wouldn't go because he was "nothing but a little man."[29]

---

[26] Letter Lucy to Rutherford, dated 1862, Papers.
[27] Letter Lucy to Rutherford, dated January 15, 1862, Papers.
[28] Letter Lucy to Rutherford, dated March 18, 1862, Papers.
[29] Letter Lucy to Rutherford, dated March 31, 1862, Papers.

In April of 1862 the war took a new, even more ominous turn. The most significant battle up until then had been the Battle of Bull Run in July 1861, which had total casualties from both sides of approximately 4,700. This was a serious clash of arms, indeed, but much worse was to come. On April 6th and 7th an incredible 24,000 total casualties were inflicted in the two days of the battle of Shiloh, which occurred at a place called Pittsburg Landing, Tennessee. This was a whole new level of intensity which shocked the nation. It was now realized by the people that this war would be even more terrible than expected, and that many more would be killed and maimed than had ever been dreamed of. The soldiers in the field were in greater danger than expected, and those at home were accordingly subjected to greater anxiety than ever.

A great deal of anxiety is felt in Cincinnati about the battle of Shiloh, but Lucy was fortunate in that she knew approximately where her husband was located, and that it was not near that battlefield. Still, the people at home were going through a national trial whether they had loved ones immediately at risk or not. It was something they all went through together, as news of fallen friends and loved ones trickled in from around the country.

A week later she reported that "the late Pittsburg battle has filled our hospitals with wounded dying men. Is it not dreadful to think of a whole Army being surprised?" The stress of it all caused Lucy's spirits to plummet. "Oh my dearest there are so many sad heart breaking things happening around us all the time that I wonder whether we can ever be the same happy people as before," she wrote Rutherford. "At times I feel that I must try and do something for our suffering soldiers. I believe that much of my sorrow and grief would be gone if I could only feel that I had eased some poor dying man."[30] In a letter to her brother Joseph she told of the many wounded men, her desire to help them, and "how my heart would warm to any woman who in suffering would tend to you."[31]

The previous month, in March of 1862, Lucy was given the opportunity to help some wounded men and she took advantage of it. On the street she passed four soldiers, two of whom were wounded and two sick, who did not have a place to stay for the night before proceeding on their journey. She had them stay in the parlor at her home. The next morning "we had a cup of coffee for them before five. I thought of you in a strange country, wounded and trying to get home," she wrote to Rutherford.[32]

The existence of the war was not something the Hayes boys could be sheltered from. The conflict was the discussion of everyone in town, the talk of

---

[30] Letter Lucy to Rutherford, dated April 22, 1862, Papers.
[31] Letter Lucy to Joseph Webb, dated April 23, 1862, Papers.
[32] Letter Lucy to Rutherford, dated May 19, 1862, Papers.

the adults with children nearby, and the children themselves would speak of it. Lucy wrote that Birchie's prayer for the last three or four weeks had included the prayer that the soldiers of their father's regiment "may not be killed, that the brave men - our men - who are fighting for our flag, may not be wounded, and if they are killed, we know, oh Lord, they are with them in Heaven."[33] "If Papa should be killed, what do you think you could do?" Birchie said one day. "Could you teach school, or would you do sewing for a living?"[34] That uncertainty and anxiety crept into the boys' minds was illustrated in May of 1863 when Webb said, "I don't think PaPa will be killed, do you mama?"[35] Would could Lucy say, but give assurances she hoped would come true?

The intensity of the times gave Lucy an emotional experience and depth she had never experienced before. "I am happily constituted, easily touched with grief, and when with kind sympathizing friends, grief is lightened " she wrote Rutherford. "I look forward to better days, but our separation is the hardest to bear and were it not for the holy glorious cause my heart would fail."[36]

"This last week has been a blue week to me - past day - all day my thoughts were with you - longing so much to see you - and feeling so unworthy of your love," she confessed one time. "Our boys brighten up life and then as I think of the uncertain future, that their life may be so sadly clouded, I cannot express to you my anxiety. But dearest, we are all well, loving you more than ever."[37]

A month after Shiloh Rutherford's regiment was ordered forward into the area of military action, and this information was known back home in Ohio. "My anxiety has been most intense for several days for I could not control my feelings on the 15th and 16th," Lucy wrote. Then she received a note from Rutherford, that he had been wounded. "Since I wrote you last I have lived a great deal," he said, describing a clash with the Confederates in which his regiment was ordered to withdraw from the field. " Could our men retreat without breaking into confusion or a rout? They retired slowly, stubbornly, in good spirits and in order! I got a scratch on the right knee, just drawing blood but spoiling my drawers. But what of that? Things were going well."[38]

"What was my joy," Lucy answered, "to receive a dispatch about eight o'clock in which but for the 'mere scratch' you are well. I do not feel so confident

---

[33] Letter Lucy to Rutherford, dated May 24, 1862, Papers.
[34] Diary, October 23, 1872.
[35] Letter Lucy to Rutherford, dated May 3, 1863, Papers.
[36] Letter Lucy to Rutherford, dated June 29, 1862, Papers.
[37] Letter Lucy to Rutherford, dated May 3, 1863, Papers.
[38] Diary, May 11, 1862.

that it is nothing more. But the lightness of heart that took the place of the heavy load is indescribable now."[39]

News of battles from many parts of the nation were the daily fare of those at home. There was no escaping it. Seven days of battles around the Confederate capital of Richmond had sent the Union Army into retreat back to Washington, ending hopes for an early end to the war. "Everything is looking dark and sad to me," Lucy wrote. "I cannot let my mind wander to future, I must keep constantly the present...there are times when every thing oppresses me."[40]

When Rutherford wrote words of cheer and encouragement to her, telling her of his love, she felt unworthy. "Your letter to me before you left V[irgini]a made me so happy, [with] the thoughts and assurances that your love was increasing always," she said, before again revealing her lack of self-esteem, "but you think of me dearest as better than the reality. If ever we are again united, it shall be my earnest constant effort to be more deserving of your love, to be more necessary to your happiness than ever. I often think of the happy future, when once more a family together, our boys loving and honors us, and think of bring happy days. God grant we may be together in old age.. Yes darling, I am getting older, but is so strange I cannot feel more than a little girl [as] when you first saw me...."[41]

In August of 1862 the Confederate Army under General Robert E. Lee struck a severe blow on the Union soldiers at the Second Battle of Bull Run. Casualties were again horrific, this time with about 22,000, or five times the number of the first battle on that same field a year before. Then Lee boldly moved his troops northward into northern Virginia and on into Maryland. The country was nearly in a panic, as Washington, Baltimore and perhaps even Philadelphia were threatened. Union troops from every nearby command were thrown into the fray, and this included Rutherford B. Hayes and the 23rd Ohio, which he now commanded.

Lucy was almost out of her mind with anxiety. "It has been almost impossible for me to composedly sit down and write, although you were constantly on my mind," she wrote. "Our anxiety has been of the most intense, and yet with all I felt you were protected. I wonder sometimes that I can endure this suspense."

With the war going so badly, she found an easy target for her blame. "My feeling toward Mr. Lincoln has day by day changed until now when he calmly sees our young men hurried into eternity for the protection of this cause, my feelings are of the most bitter kind," she wrote. "What does he care - oh is it to

[39] Letter Lucy to Rutherford, dated May 17, 1862, Papers.
[40] Letter Lucy to Rutherford, dated July 21, 1862, Papers.
[41] Letter Lucy to Rutherford, dated August 29, 1862, Papers.

continue so till our noble army is completely cut to pieces."[42] So many people across America felt the same way.

The huge armies maneuvered around each other through the countryside of three states, seeking the best advantage in the battle to come. All knew that the coming encounter would be titanic in scope and in importance. Another Union defeat could be the end of the war effort in the North. In a significant but still preliminary encounter, the armies of Union General McClellan and Confederate General Lee clashed on September 14, 1862, in western Maryland in a battle that became known as South Mountain.

The 23rd Regiment of Ohio Volunteers under Colonel Rutherford B. Hayes was there and in the midst of the fighting. Hayes ordered a charge and his men moved forward, breaking the enemy before them and driving them out of the woods. "Our men halted at a fence near the edge of the woods and kept up a brisk fire upon the enemy, who were sheltering themselves behind stone walls and fences near the top of the hill, beyond a cornfield in front of our position," Hayes recorded. "Just as I gave the command to charge I felt a stunning blow and found a musket ball had struck my left arm just above the elbow. Fearing that an artery might be cut, I asked a soldier near me to tie my handkerchief above the wound. I soon felt weak, faint, and sick at the stomach. I laid down and was pretty comfortable. I was perhaps twenty feet behind the line of my men... [A] few moments after I first laid down, seeing something going wrong [in the battle] and feeling a little easier, I got up and began to give directions about things; but after a few moments, getting very weak, I again laid down."

Battle wounds were a very dangerous thing in the Civil War. It was easy for one not to realize the danger of a wound, and for even a relatively minor injury to turn deadly. Hayes knew this, and the thought crossed his mind that he might be mortally wounded. "While I was lying down I had [a] considerable talk with a wounded [Confederate] soldier lying near me," he wrote. Thinking of Lucy, his sons, and friends, he quickly scratched out some words to them. "I gave him messages for my wife and friends in case I should not get up."

It turned out that Rutherford's wound was not mortal, and he did get up. As soon as he was able to do so later in the day, he sent telegraphs to Lucy, Uncle Birchard and others. His brother-in-law, Dr. Joseph Webb, dressed his wound and his orderly, Harvey Carrington, cared for him.[43] He was more fortunate than many men so badly wounded in that his brother in law did not amputate his arm.

---

[42] Letter Lucy to Rutherford, dated September 1862, Papers.
[43] Diary, September 14, 1862.

Rutherford was taken to the home of Captain Jacob Rudy in Middletown, Maryland, where he was given a bed and shelter.

On September 17, 1862, the bloodiest single day of the entire Civil War occurred. The great armies grappled in a huge battle at Antietam, Maryland, the sounds of which could be heard miles away by Rutherford at the Rudy home. On that one day some 27,000 Northerners and Southerners were made casualties of war. The battle was a tactical draw as neither army drove the other from the field, but it was a rare strategic Union victory as the battle halted Lee's northward drive. In its wake, the countryside was awash with thousands upon thousands of wounded men needing shelter and care.

It is interesting to note that this Union success in Maryland, such as it was, gave President Lincoln the battlefield victory he wanted as a backdrop to issuing the Emancipation Proclamation. That document, of course, announced the freeing of slaves in the rebel states, and led ultimately to the abolition of all African slavery everywhere in the United States. Rutherford and Lucy Hayes played a part in this. Their joint sacrifice of putting Rutherford into the Army and into the war in that very campaign, along with like contributions from so many homes across the North, made that result - the Emancipation Proclamation - possible. Rutherford put his life in harm's way, and he was in fact harmed, to help make this happen.

When Rutherford was wounded in battle Lucy was not in Cincinnati, but in Chillicothe visiting family. As a result the message did not find her until four days later. On September the dreaded news that Lucy had hoped never to receive was in her hand - Rutherford had been shot in battle. "I am here, come to me. I shall not lose my arm," said a cryptic telegraphic message from Rutherford.[44] One can easily imagine the emotions that must have swept through Lucy then and throughout her journey to him. Indications on the telegram were that it was sent from Washington, and Lucy made immediate plans to go. The boys were placed with family and she was on her way.

She arrived in Washington on the twenty first and began frantically searching the numerous hospitals around the capital city, but never finding Rutherford. She discovered some wounded men from the 23rd Ohio who confirmed that Rutherford had been wounded and was back in Maryland. Lucy went to Frederick where she found her brother, Dr. Joseph Webb, and he took her straight to her husband. She finally found her beloved among the thousands of injured men

---

[44] Geer, p. 57.

across the state. "Well," said Rutherford in jest when she arrived, "you thought you would visit Washington and Baltimore."[45]

Lucy gave Rutherford the loving care he needed, and they were glad to be together at this important time in their lives. Sometimes she would visit other wounded men to cheer and comfort them, and then return to Rutherford in tears from the experience.[46] Lucy "visits the wounded and is much interested in them," Rutherford wrote to his mother. "I am doing well, and shall probably get home in three or four weeks. Many of the wounded are starting home, and all hope to get leave to go before they return to service. I am not suffering much. The weariness from lying abed is the chief annoyance."[47]

After a couple of weeks they were able, in the company of several other wounded men from the regiment, to take the train back home to Cincinnati. Once they returned to Ohio, Rutherford recovered well. Lucy had an attack of diphtheria at the end of October, leaving her unable to swallow or speak for a period of time.[48]

His arm recovered slowly, it became the unhappy duty of Rutherford to return to his regiment. He did not fully recover for a year, but was able to return to his duties. Surely it was a day that Lucy and the boys dreaded. It turned out to be an unusual leave taking. On Saturday, November 22, 1862, the sad goodbyes were said, and Rutherford boarded an Ohio River steamboat. A few miles away the boat ran aground on a sand bar and could not proceed until the water rose, which would be some time. Rutherford got off the ship a took a streetcar back home, surprising his delighted wife and sons. Leaving the next day, the boat was still aground and he returned. The routine was followed twice more. "Bid good-bye to Lucy, boys, and all, four times on different days," Rutherford wrote in his diary.[49]

Back in the military zone, Rutherford was promoted to Brigadier General and given command of the First Brigade of the Second Kanawha Division in what just been admitted to the Union as West Virginia. In those days before motorized travel on hard road surfaces, war usually ground to a halt in cold weather as the armies went into winter camp. This was true in the Revolutionary War (as in Valley Forge) and it was true again in the Civil War. This presented an opportunity, never known in the twentieth century, for families to make extended visits to officers in camp.

[45] Ari Hoogdenboom, *Rutherford B Hayes: One of the Good Colonels*, Abilene, Texas: McWhiney Foundation Press, 1999, p. 57.
[46] Diary, September 26, 1862.
[47] Ibid.
[48] Diary, October 31, 1862.
[49] Diary, November 24 and December 2, 1862.

Rutherford sent word for Lucy to come for the winter, and to bring the older boys with her. Of the previous twenty months, Lucy and Rutherford had been separated for seventeen. On January 24, 1863, Lucy arrived at Camp Reynolds near Charleston, West Virginia. She brought Birch and Webb with her, making an unusual war experience to modern eyes. The younger boys, Ruddy and Joseph, were left in the care of Lucy's mother. "We shall enjoy the log cabin life very much," Rutherford wrote his own mother. "[T]he boys are especially happy, running about where there is so much new to be seen."[50]

Lucy wrote to Uncle Birchard that "it is very muddy. I have not been out through the Camp but from our Cabin we have a beautiful view and the roaring of the [river] waters all make it very delightful."[51] Before they left for home on March 21st, Rutherford noted in his diary that the boys "rowed skiffs, fished, built dams, sailed little ships, played cards, and enjoyed camp life generally.[52] War was very different then!

As soon as she was home Lucy wrote Rutherford, letting him know they had safely arrived. On the way she was helped with the boys by the kindness of people on the steamboat. She was very appreciative and tried to learn a lesson from it for her own conduct. "I always meet with kindness and will always try more than ever to return what I always receive." Reaching home, she and Birch were near crying for the hurt of missing their husband and father.[53]

Being back home again meant the same life of rumors of battles, anxieties and loneliness. Having seen the dreadful ravages of battle wounds by her experience near Antietam, she had a more realistic and terrible knowledge of what war was really about. When she learned that in Rutherford's area communication was cut off and the river was in the possession of the Rebels, she wrote him that "the imagination has full play - all the terrible casualties are before the mind." Again she put on a brave front, assuring her husband that she was a worthy soldier's wife. "[D]o not imagine that when I am terrified and anxious I publish it to friends," she concluded.[54]

In the summer of 1863 Rutherford's regiment was safely back in the vicinity of Charleston, West Virginia, which was within a reasonable distance of Ohio. There were no immediate plans for moving into the war zone, so General Hayes sent for his wife. On June 15th Lucy, her mother and Birch, Webb, Ruddy and little Joseph all arrived at Camp White. They were able to find a temporary home

---

[50] Diary, January 25, 1863.
[51] Letter Lucy to Uncle Birchard, dated January 25, 1863, Papers.
[52] Diary March 15, 1863.
[53] Letter Lucy to Rutherford, dated March 24, 1863, Papers.
[54] Letter Lucy to Rutherford, dated April 8, 1863, Papers.

a short distance from Rutherford's tent in a little cottage on the river bank. It was an idyllic place.

After a few happy days of visiting, Joseph became ill will dysentery and died just after noon on June 24th. "Poor little darling!" Rutherford wrote in his diary the next day. "A sweet, bright boy, 'looked like his father,' but with large, handsome blue eyes much like Webb's. Teething, dysentery, and brain affected, the diseases. He died without suffering; lay on the table in our room in the Quarrier cottage, surrounded by white roses and buds all the afternoon, and was sent to Cincinnati in care of Corporal Schirmes...this morning." The father honestly stated that "I have seen so little of him, born since the war, that I do not realize a loss; but his mother, and still more his grandmother, lose their little dear companion, and are very much afflicted."[55]

When she departed a few days later, Rutherford noted that Lucy was remarkably cheerful despite her devastating loss. "But on leaving today without him," he wrote in his diary, "she burst into tears on seeing a little child on the boat."[56]

July of 1863 was the turning point in the war. General Lee had again taken his Confederate army northward, into Maryland and this time on into Pennsylvania. It was the cause of the greatest consternation in Washington. The day Lucy and her three boys left camp on their sad journey homeward was the first day of the battle of Gettysburg, which ended with the General Lee's army again heading southward. Further west in Ohio, the rumors were rife that Confederate General John Hunt Morgan and his cavalry raiders would invade the state.

Morgan and his men crossed the Ohio River from Kentucky into Indiana, then moved eastward. On July 13th they made it to Harrison, Ohio, just twenty-five miles from Cincinnati. Lucy wrote to Uncle Birchard that "we have had so constant an excitement about Morgan that it has been almost impossible for me to write. Today the shops are closed, and rumors are all about that Morgan is endeavoring to force his way back. He is reported with in twelve miles, and troops are expected at noon from Cincinnati."[57] Morgan never made it, being surrounded and captured by a Union army sent in from Kentucky.

Having been at the very site in West Virginia, when Rutherford wrote that his regiment was back where it had been, Lucy knew just what he was talking about. "You are back at Charleston - Camp White - I can close my eyes and be with you-

[55] Diary, June 25, 1863.
[56] Diary, July 1, 1863.
[57] Letter Lucy to Uncle Birchard, dated July 22, 1863, Papers.

your tent is before me," she wrote him, "and I can imagine at times that I am with you."[58]

In October she really was with him at Camp White. She left Webb and Ruddy with her mother and Birch went with his namesake uncle to Spiegel Grove in Fremont. Rutherford explained to his mother than in the uncertainty of the military situation then prevailing, he could not make arrangements for his entire family to come as they had before. "In the meantime Lucy is enjoying a visit here," he reported. "We have a number of agreeable ladies in camp, and are making pleasant acquaintances among the citizens."[59]

Lucy missed her boys and wrote to them, telling them she was lonely without them and hoping that they could soon join their parents at winter camp. "This morning as I sit by my window...I am thinking of my darling boys and would like to peep in for a few moments."[60] On October 21st Lucy left for home with her brother Joseph to gather up the boys, rent out the house in Cincinnati, and return with the whole family to Camp White. A month later Lucy returned with Webb, Ruddy and Grandma Webb.

"We are all here living very comfortably. Webb and Ruddy are learning lessons daily," Rutherford wrote to his mother. Explaining why she had not received a letter from Lucy, he said that "Lucy writes very few letters to anybody and avoids it when she can. She finds a sympathizing friend on this subject in Mrs. Comly, who dislikes it equally. When I am with Lucy, I do the writing."[61] That was true. Once she had written to Rutherford that "writing is not my forte but loving is."[62] But there was, of course, more to it than that. As we have seen, Lucy had no great attachment to her mother-in-law and probably did not want to communicate with her.

Birch, who was not with them at winter camp, was missed. "It is a long while my dear boy to have you from me ," she wrote him. "I wonder if you think of Ma ma and Grand Ma as often as they do of you." Moving on to more mundane things, she said only what a mother can say. "[D]on't forget to keep your teeth clean. Are the others growing down right?[63]

The weather at the camp turned cold, but the Hayes family was undeterred in enjoying the situation. The "had "good sleighing about ten days. The river was

---

[58] Letter Lucy to Rutherford, dated August 2, 1863, Papers.
[59] Diary, October 10, 1863.
[60] Letter Lucy to Birchie, dated October 10, 1863, Papers.
[61] Diary, December 3, 1863.
[62] Letter Lucy to Rutherford, dated June 4, 1862, Papers.
[63] Letter Lucy to Birchie, dated December 18, 1863, Papers.

closed, cutting us off completely from the civilized world. Provisions were pretty plenty, however, and we felt independent of the weather."[64]

At the end of January Lucy finally got off a letter to "Mother Hayes." "We are living in an old home that years ago must have been highly improved, "she wrote. "Even now the garden is full of choice roses and flowers of various kinds. The boys Webb and Rud are perfectly happy, hunting around for the first appearance of the little plants... We have a good deal to occupy our time, a little visiting each day, watching the arrival of the boats with our Companies returning, some sewing, a little sweeping and dusting, but no housekeeping. The boys have a little dog which is a fine playfellow for them and a great favorite of mine as he shows a decided preference for me."[65] The Winter Quarters consisted of a village of board houses with an upper room for children to sleep in, large stone fireplaces with chimneys in the center of the house.

By the end of April the weather and roads had improved and the armies were preparing for a fourth years of warfare. It was time for the wives and children to go home, and for the great carnage of war to begin anew. The year of 1864 would be a terrible one, with casualties inflicted at the greatest rate ever. The new Union commander, General Ulysses S. Grant, began to press General Lee's Confederates and would not let go, so the fighting went on and on. Grant lost more casualties than Lee had men in his entire army, and yet the fighting still went on. Lincoln and Grant were willing to do whatever it took to end the war, and this was what it took.

"After weeks of great anxiety I received your dispatch," Lucy wrote Rutherford. "I do not think you know the great joy it is to hear so speedily that you are safe and well... It was sad news to hear so many true noble souls had fallen. Every where are weeping mourning souls, yet I am spared. I cannot tell you the sorrow and sympathy I have for our mourning friends."[66]

Doing what little she could, Lucy made a battle flag and sent it to Rutherford's regiment. When she received word that it was delivered to the men without their knowing it was from her, she was upset. "Now about the flag," she wrote sternly. "I want our soldiers to know that I sent it to them. It is something like the Apples I sent to Capt Gilmore's men - I don't think they ever knew it. Well enough of that - let them know how near they are to me, that not a day passes that our gallant soldiers are not remembered by me." They found out that the flag was from Lucy Hayes, the wife of the general.

[64] Diary, January 17, 1864.
[65] Letter Lucy to Mother Hayes, dated January 31, 1864, Papers.
[66] Letter Lucy to Rutherford, dated May 26, 1864, Papers.

When Lucy received word that her flag had gone into battle she was proud of it. "The Color Sergant [sic] loves the flag. My heart warmed towards him," she wrote. "I can imagine what his feeling must be towards it after having borne it in battle." She then wanted to know more about him, and made an interesting comment about not being forgotten. "Do you know him or the guard personally. If you do I shall feel that the Flag is nearer to me, that I will not be forgotten." She wanted so badly to be a part of the soldiers, of the war effort. "It is a very pleasant recollection to me that our soldiers felt kindly towards me."[67]

The unrelenting battles in Virginia continued. "I have no news to write - nothing in our little quiet town," Lucy wrote. "I don't believe we think talk or care for any thing but the war, and many and fervent prayers are offered that it will soon close. Good bye dearest remember me to my many friends in the Twenty third - God preserve you all."[68] The fighting continued in September and Lucy tried t keep up her spirits and confidence. "You have passed through many dangers, in the last three years," she wrote Rutherford, "and my hopeful heart thinks of all and still feels it may be so again-[69]

In Ohio the name of General Rutherford B. Hayes began to be promoted as a Republican candidate for Congress. This was not an unwelcome prospect for Rutherford, but the timing of it was impossible. "Your suggestion about getting a furlough to take to the stump was certainly made without reflection," he wrote disgustedly to an overly-enthusiastic supporter. "An officer fit for duty who at this crisis would abandon his post to electioneer for a seat in Congress ought to be scalped. You may feel perfectly sure I shall do no such thing."[70] That turned out to be the best political speech he ever gave. He was elected to Congress in November 1864. At that time, however, representatives elected did not take their seats for thirteen months, in December 1865.

On September 29, 1864, a fifth son was born to Lucy and Rutherford. "Our boy is nearly three weeks old," Lucy told the father. "I sometimes think you may not have heard of the darling's arrival- while I was confined to my bed my great happiness was your letters.... Our boy is a fine large child- weighed 10 lbs at his birth- no little stranger was ever so warmly welcomed by Uncles and Cousins."[71]

The three older boys called the baby "Joe" after the baby that had died, which was a common thing in the nineteenth century. "I find that name seems to bring our dear little one that is gone back to me again. Our dear little Joe seems to be

[67] Letter Lucy to Rutherford, dated September 8, 1864, Papers.
[68] Letter Lucy to Rutherford, dated June 26, 1864, Papers.
[69] Letter Lucy to Rutherford, dated September 13, 1864, Papers.
[70] Diary, August 24, 1864.
[71] Letter Lucy to Rutherford, dated October 29, 1864, Papers.

with us again, but I have told the children we must try and call him baby till we hear from papa."[72] Papa, it turned out, did not want the name "Joseph" again, but instead named him George Crook Hayes after his favorite Army corps commander. Like the earlier son, however, George suffered badly from the colic.

Lucy became extremely worried when Rutherford's brigade was sent to be within the area commanded by Ulysses S. Grant. His reputation for success was, for her, overwhelmed by his record of very high casualties. She was relieved shortly thereafter when Rutherford was able to come home in January 1865 for a month's leave. This gave him the chance to get to know his new little son and help Lucy, who was suffering from a severe attack of rheumatism since George's birth.

General Hayes had the opportunity to go to Washington for the March 4, 1865, inauguration of President Abraham Lincoln for a second term in office. Lucy was to go with him, but the continual discomfort of the rheumatism prevented it and Rutherford went without her. She missed Lincoln's great speech, in which he called for the nation to move forward "with malice toward none, with charity for all." The President in the final months of the war had become transformed in the mind of the public to a man of gigantic virtue and strength. Lucy felt this transformation as well. Rutherford wrote back to Lucy that the new Vice President, Andrew Johnson, had spoiled the event with his drunkenness.

A month later Lucy heard the wonderful news of the surrender of Confederate General Robert E. Lee on April 9th. After four long and difficult years - difficult for the nation and for the Hayes family personally - the war was finally ending. Great celebrations broke out spontaneously throughout the North, and surely no one was gladder that the war over than Lucy Hayes.

The happy news quickly turned unhappy five days later when President Lincoln was murdered by John Wilkes Booth at a theater in Washington, D.C. "When I heard first yesterday morning of the awful tragedy at Washington," Rutherford wrote Lucy, "I was pained and shocked to a degree I have never before experienced.... The Nation's great joy turned suddenly to a still greater sorrow! A ruler tested and proved in every way, and in every way found equal to the occasion, to be exchanged for a new man whose ill-omened beginning made the Nation hang its head. Lincoln for Johnson! The work of reconstruction requiring so much statesmanship just begun! The calamity to Mr. Lincoln; in a personal point of view, so uncalled for a fate! - so undeserved, so unprovoked!"

Both Lucy and Rutherford became angry with those who wanted a gentle peace, though this was what Lincoln had favored. The President had wanted to

---

[72] Letter Lucy to Rutherford, dated October 18, 1864, Papers.

welcome the Southern states and people back into the Union with as little difficulty as possible, but his murder made Northerners sour on being merciful for their Southern brethren. "It is possible that a greater degree of severity in dealing with the Rebellion may be ordered, and that may be for the best," wrote Rutherford angrily.[73] Lucy agreed. "I am sick of the endless talk of forgiveness, taking them back like brothers," she wrote.[74] It was not like her to say such a thing, but four years of war and sacrifice takes a toll on one's charity toward those causing the war. "The mind can hardly be brought to think [of] a man or a country so fallen as to sacrifice their last friend," she said of the South and the murder of the President. "Mercy was his error and oh how much we need justice."[75] Her opinion was no different from millions of Americans.

---

[73] Diary, April 16, 1865.
[74] Letter Lucy to Rutherford, dated April 17, 1865, Papers.
[75] Letter Lucy to Uncle John Joseph Cook, dated May 3, 1865, Papers.

Lucy at age 16.

Rutherford and Lucy Webb Hayes, wedding portrait, December 30th, 1852.

Lucy holding oldest son Birchard Austin Hayes, around 1854.

The family at Spiegel Grove, l. to r., Birchard Austin Hayes, his wife Mary Sherman Hayes, the President, Scott R. Hayes, Rutherford Platt Hayes, Lucy, Fanny Hayes, and Webb Cook Hayes.

Lucy Hayes in White House Conservatory with Carrie Davis (daughter of artist Theodore Davis, who created the Hayes White House China), Scott Hayes and Fanny Hayes.

Formal presidential portrait, 1877.

Lucy wearing one of her husband's old hats, feeds her pigeons, Spiegel Grove, 1888.

Chapter 5

CONGRESS AND THE GOVERNOR'S MANSION

With the war over at last, life did not immediately return to normal for the Hayes family. The surrender of General Lee did not alone end the war, as each separate Confederate army had to surrender on its own. It was not until May 26th that the last major command west of the Mississippi River surrendered, and only then could the great armies be disbanded and the soldiers be sent home. In early June Rutherford resigned his command as a general in the United States Army, and returned to Ohio.

Prior to his leaving the military Lucy joined Rutherford for his final days. On May 23 and 24, 1865, they both attended the Grand Review of the Army in Washington. This was one of the most spectacular scenes of the Civil War, a giant celebration of triumph as the great victorious armies paraded in review before the President and other officials of government. The infantry in its thousands, the cavalry on its magnificent horses, and the artillery with its cannons, all passed by. Lucy watched President Andrew Johnson through binoculars. She thought him "a fine noble looking man who impresses you with the feeling of honesty and sincerity." She peered over at the commander of all the armies, Ulysses S. Grant, thinking him ""noble" and "unassuming." Now that the fighting was over, Grant's reputation for high casualties no longer threatened her husband's safety.[1]

Then they returned home, but even then life was not as it once was. The house in Cincinnati had been leased out since early 1864 when Lucy and the boys went to join Rutherford in winter encampment, and it was not until October that it would again be available for occupancy. After her return from camp Lucy had been living in a rented cottage in Chillicothe. Between June and October, with

---

[1] Geer, p. 78.

Rutherford back home, the family resided at Maria Webb's home and at Spiegel Grove in Fremont. At last, in October the entire family - husband, wife, and four sons - all moved back into their own home. This day had been a long time coming.

Normalcy lasted only a very short time, though, as Rutherford went on to Washington, D.C., as the Representative for the second district of Ohio. He arrived there at the end of November, taking the oath of office the following month. As a Congressman Rutherford was not as vengeful toward the South as many of his colleagues, and his comparatively conciliatory ways placed him in opposition to the extreme radicals who sought to punish the South with a harsh reconstruction. He took the train back home to Cincinnati for Christmas.

When he returned in January 1866, Lucy joined him. "Lucy got here Thursday evening and is, in a quiet way, enjoying life here very much," Rutherford wrote. "We have been as yet to no receptions or parties, but find plenty to interest and amuse in the public buildings, courts, and Congress. The weather is bright and bracing. Lucy and I went to the preaching of Mr. Boynton at the Capitol today and heard a good sound talk to a large fine audience. The House makes a beautiful place for worship."[2]

They did attend a reception for General Grant, where they made an effort to be the very first people there. They were successful in this, being the first to speak with General and Mrs. Grant, and then spent the evening watch the many notables who came afterward. Lucy would go to the visitor's gallery at the House of Representatives almost daily, following the proceedings and experiencing in her way what Rutherford was experiencing as a freshman Congressman.[3] Sometimes she would go over to the Senate and watch what was happening there, and seeing the famous men of the day. She decided that she did not have a high opinion of President Andrew Johnson and his policies. On February 27th Lucy headed back home to her boys, who had again been distributed among the extended family.

In Cincinnati on May 24, 1866, twenty-month-old little George Hayes dies. "Our darling little George died today at half-past one p. m.," Rutherford sadly informed his mother, Sophia. "He was attacked with scarlet fever three or four weeks ago. After a week or two we thought him out of immediate danger, and I returned to Washington. A week ago he seemed so much worse that I was dispatched that he was sinking. I came home a week ago tomorrow. I found him low and was prepared for the worst. He was a very handsome child; abundant waving light hair; very large blue eyes and a broad, full forehead."[4] "My chief

---

[2] Diary, January 21, 1866.
[3] Diary, February 4, 1866.
[4] Diary, May 24, 1866.

consolation is found in thinking of the good ones we have left," he told Lucy, referring to Birch, Webb and Rud."[5] Lucy, of course, was grieving. She composed a written memorial of young George, and sent it to Rutherford, who had returned to Washington.

By the middle of summer, Lucy decided not to return to Washington as originally planned, probably because she did not want to leave her boys behind after George's death. Rutherford's absence to the capital city had become a strain to him, and undoubtedly to Lucy as well. First there was four years of war, and now another year in Congress, making five years in which they had been more apart than together. "I don't believe I told you my feelings when I got your letter that you were not coming to be with me the rest of this session," Rutherford wrote. "I feel more and more the desire to be with you all the time. Oh, an occasional absence of a week or two is a good thing to give one the happiness of meeting again, but this living apart is in all ways bad. We have had our share of separate life during the four years of war. There is nothing in the small ambition of Congressional life, or in the gratified vanity which it sometimes affords, to compensate for separation from you. We must manage to live together hereafter. I can't stand this, and will not."[6]

Four months after the death of her son, Lucy lost her mother, Maria Webb, as well. Maria was the only parent Lucy had ever known, and her passing on September 14, 1866, was a huge loss. The next month Rutherford's mother, Sophia Hayes, also died.

Following this unhappy year of loneliness and death, Rutherford and Lucy decided to take a break at Christmas, going south to New Orleans for the holidays. They toured Tennessee, visiting battlefields they had heard about. "Good times, banquets, etc., etc., at Knoxville, Chattanooga, and here [Nashville]," Rutherford wrote to Uncle Birchard. "We visit the battlefields and mix with the leading Rebels in a friendly and sensible way. We go to Memphis tonight. Stay all day Christmas and go to New Orleans. Lucy is doing her best and enjoying it hugely."[7]

Rutherford especially liked meeting with his former foes. He spoke with them boldly of Negro suffrage and radical reconstruction, and the Southerners would politely disagree. He obtained a signature of Confederate General Pierre G. T. Beauregard and sent to Uncle Birchard. "Lucy very happy," he reported in another letter.

---

[5] Diary, June 6, 1866.
[6] Diary, June 17, 1866.
[7] Diary, December 24, 1866.

After his re-election to a second term in 1866, there began to be talk of running Congressman Hayes as the Republican candidate for Governor of Ohio. Rutherford wasn't sure what to say to it, but wrote Uncle Birchard that "the truth as I now see it: I don't particularly enjoy Congressional life. I have no ambition for Congressional reputation or influence--not a particle. I would like to be out of it creditably." Maybe becoming Governor would be that respectable way out of Washington and back home, and he was agreeable to it if the people of his district who sent him to Congress approved of it.[8] Meanwhile Lucy joined him in Washington for the 1867 session.

Although he had decided in February not to run, in June Rutherford was nominated anyway for Governor of Ohio by the Republican state convention. At the conclusion of business the next month he resigned his seat in Congress and returned to Ohio for the political campaign. He had found his way out.

In November of 1867 he was elected Governor. In those days of less government, the position was not as burdensome as it now is. "I am enjoying the new office. It strikes me at a guess as the pleasantest I have ever had," he wrote Uncle Birchard, who undoubtedly was very proud of his nephew. " Not too much hard work, plenty of time to read, good society, etc.," he concluded.[9]

The family now had to leave Cincinnati and move into the governor's mansion in the state capital of Columbus. Lucy was immediately thrust to the top of the social scene in that city and in Ohio as a whole, and she enjoyed it. She loved people, inviting them over for dinner, and being involved in what was going on. As a means of encouraging better conditions and care, she toured institutions for the poor, the disabled, and the disadvantaged. She successfully urged the establishment of a home for the orphans of soldiers, and the providing of state services to students with hearing and speaking problems.

Lucy's child-bearing years were not over. Frances "Fanny" Hayes was born in Cincinnati on September 2, 1867, just two months before Rutherford's election as governor. Of her eight children, this was the only daughter. She was named for Rutherford's sister. Scott Russell Hayes was born in Columbus on February 8, 1871. He weighed eleven pounds and Lucy has slow in recovering from childbirth.

While between terms in the governorship, Rutherford and Lucy had their last child, Manning Force Hayes. He was born August 1, 1873, in Fremont, and named for General Manning Force, another of Rutherford's compatriots in arms. She was very weak in the weeks following this last birth. Lucy was again very

---

[8] Diary, February 2, 1867.
[9] Diary, January 17, 1868.

weak for some time after the birth. She had borne eight children over twenty years, a considerable physical feat for any woman. Young Manning died of dysentery a year later on August 28, 1874, on Lucy's 42nd birthday. For a third time Lucy had the heartache of a mother losing a child to death. He was buried in the Oak Wood Cemetery in Fremont. "With all out changes and sorrows," Lucy wrote her son Webb, "a happy and blessed family we have been and are."[10]

In 1870 Rutherford observed that Lucy, who stood five feet four a half inches, was gaining weight, leaving her young figure behind forever. "Lucy is gaining flesh and color again, and never looked more charmingly in my eyes than last evening," he said in April.[11] On June 3rd he dropped another comment: "Lucy fattens a little which improves her good looks."[12] Then on December 31, 1871, he concluded the year with the observation that "Lucy is handsome, ages slowly. and gaining flesh with years, is a fine matronly looking woman."[13] The Victorian era was nothing like the youth-obsessed, too-thin social culture that exists in the United States of today, but even then these heavy handed comments by Rutherford must have been an unwelcome verbalization as far as the subject (Lucy) was concerned. One wonders if Lucy ever read them herself, and what she thought. The truth of it was that the years added to the frame of Rutherford as well.

On January 1, 1872, Governor Hayes prepared to leave office. A reception was held, and the Hayes left on a happy note. "Altogether, a happy New Year's day," Rutherford wrote in his dairy. "Lucy had about one hundred callers and enjoyed it vastly."

Lucy continued with her interest in politics and government. The Republican Party was divided over the re-nomination of President Ulysses S. Grant for a second term, which many did not want. His closeness to big money capitalists and the political cronyism and corruption he allowed to exist caused many to leave the regular party. These political dissidents formed what was called the Liberal Republican Party, which met in Cincinnati in May 1872 to nominate a candidate for president to run against Grant. Lucy was very interested in this and attended the convention with her friend, Emma Foote and some other ladies of the town. It nominated New York City newspaper editor Horace Greeley for President, which turned out to be very poor choice.

---

[10] Lewis L. Gould, Editor, *American First Ladies: Their Lives and Their Legacy*, New York: Garland Publishing, Inc., 1996, p. 223.
[11] Diary, April 22, 1870.
[12] Diary, June 3, 1870.
[13] Diary, December 31, 1871.

Rutherford, a Republican political heavyweight in Ohio as a former governor, did not attend the insurgent convention. In fact, the following month he was a delegate to the Republican National Convention in Philadelphia, which nominated Grant for another term. The thought probably never crossed his mind that four years hence, he - Rutherford B. Hayes - would himself be nominated for President at the next national convention.

Back in Ohio there was talk about nominated Rutherford for Congress again. "I do not want to return to Congress," he wrote in his diary, "and, of course, do not wish to be nominated."[14] On the other hand, he confided that if were nominated he would not feel free to decline to run. So in August he was nominated, and he decided to make the race. "The whole thing is, I confess, flattering," he finally admitted in his diary.[15] The year of 1872, however, witnessed a Democratic-Liberal Republican tide in Ohio, which swept all before it. Rutherford was, along with many other Republicans defeated. He felt a little sting by his failure to carry Cincinnati.

In October, just before the election, Fanny was involved in a serious horse accident that scared her parents. "Her accident was a very dangerous one," Rutherford wrote. "She hung by one foot in the stirrup, the pony dashing among the trees. Her escape was a marvel. She was left senseless several hours. But no fever followed, and no serious harm. I look at her with a feeling of gratitude. She is so improved and has such an affectionate disposition."[16] Undoubtedly, Lucy felt the same way.

Rutherford's defeat in Cincinnati perhaps set the stage psychologically for the next step he and Lucy took, which was to move permanently away to Fremont. Cincinnati had been their home for more than twenty years, and they surely had some feelings of trepidation in the change. But Spiegel Grove was a wonderful place to live, and by the spring of 1873 they were there. "We now are here for good. My return to Fremont after an absence of over twenty-four years is exceedingly pleasant," Rutherford wrote I his diary. "I can now be useful to my town, neighbors, and friends. There is a general feeling of pleasure at my return."[17] Lucy loved the place, too, with its fine house and extended acreage for privacy.

Ever the writer, Rutherford began a journal of his improvements at Spiegel Grove. "My Uncle, Sardis Birchard, has given me his favorite place 'Spiegel Grove' about thirty acres South of John Street and North West of Buckland

---

[14] Diary, July 25, 1872.
[15] Diary, August 7, 1872.
[16] Diary, October 6, 1872.
[17] Diary, May 4, 1873.

Avenue," he wrote on April 22, 1873. "I am now beginning to fit it up for my home. The rest of this book is to be used in jotting down items in regard to it, and to the improvements to be made." Over the years Rutherford and Lucy made vast improvements to the home, making it their own, and it was still under expansion when Lucy died there years later. They planted apple, peach and pear trees which gave a crop of fruit each year, and many decorative trees. This was something in which Lucy was interested and in which she participated. She directed the planting of the plum trees and the transplanting of lilacs by workers, and personally planted flowering shrubs. It was active and exciting time, building a home for the remainder of their lives.

Illustrating the lifestyle that Lucy and Rutherford lived, he wrote in his beginning entry some information that illustrated the lifestyle they had. They employed an Irish groundsman named Edward who had trouble with drunkenness and three "girls," one of whom spoke no English. They had two horses, one of which was twenty-two years old, two cows, and an old dog named "Major," plus many cats and sheep.[18]

Lucy obtained a copy of a book by Harriet Beecher Stowe called "Old Town Folks. " It was a story about life in New England, and was Stowe's most popular book since "Uncle Tom's Cabin" in the 1850s. Over the summer of 1873 Lucy read it aloud to the kids "with great unction to the boys, who rest from their labors and laugh and listen in a comfortable way. It is very jolly. As good as a play. She says the good grandmother is like her grandmother."[19]

"The twenty-first of January, 1874, was a dismal day, "Rutherford wrote in his diary. "The fog in Fremont was the heaviest ever known." The weather, however, was not what depressed him. His beloved Uncle Birchard was seriously ill and that day became more so. "His voice continued natural and strong and his head clear until he died about an hour after the attack began. He was cheerful, kind, and friendly and affectionate. He said he was glad I could be with him. I held his right hand." Uncle Birchard was humorous to the end. "'I shall soon see Fanny and Mrs. Valette; that is, if I go to the right place (this with a playful smile) and I think I shall.' And so with pleasant talk until the moment when a single spasm brought the end. A beautiful close to a beautiful life."[20]

Uncle Birchard had been a loving and giving benefactor to Rutherford and Lucy, and now he left his large fortune solely to his nephew. Rutherford and Lucy were now the masters of Spiegel Grove. They busied themselves making the

---

[18] "Our Home" book of entries by Rutherford B. Hayes, transcribed by George Sinclair and John Ransom, 1997, Rutherford B. Hayes Presidential Center.
[19] Diary, July 2, 1873.
[20] Diary, January 29, 1874.

splendid house and grounds their own, remaking it, improving it, adding to it, just as they pleased. "We have been busy with our improvements of grounds and house for more than three months. We are now at the end of the first installment - kitchen, range, buttery, etc."[21]

On Thanksgiving Day of 1873 there was a large gathering at Spiegel Grove, with about twenty people seated around the table. "Our Winnie, colored cook, outdid herself," Rutherfrod recorded. "Three turkeys, large and well roasted, one not carved, one ham and a dish of fried oysters, bread, rolls, finely cut cheese, mashed potatoes, stewed tomatoes, cranberries."[22]

The winter was a very cold one. When it thawed in March with temperatures up to 70 degrees, the roads turned to bottomless mud. They put Fanny and Scott each on a sled with an umbrella on the pond with clear and smooth ice, and watched them glide as the wind drove them.[23]

"We are living happily; never more so," Rutherford wrote three days later. He surveyed the family that Lucy and he had made for themselves. "Scott Russell's promotion to pants has been the event of the last week. Little Fanny is healthy, bright, and good. She does not take to 'book larnin.' But that will come in time, no doubt. Birch takes more and more interest in the law. I think he will be a good lawyer. Ruddy, at Lansing, says he is homesick. He repeats it three times in the same letter. But his letters are cheerful. He says he works at chopping three hours daily. Webb writes good letters from Cornell. Lucy is healthy, and as she grows older preserves her beauty."

Then came the diary bombshell that hopefully Lucy never saw: "She is large but not unwieldy." Photographs show that this was an over-statement of reality. "The only drawback," he continued in speaking of Lucy, "is her frequent attacks of sick headaches. Perhaps twice a month she suffers for a day or two." Finally came his own admission: "I too am healthy, getting a little too fat for comfort. The independence [from] all political and other bother is a happiness."[24]

Independence from politics was destined not to last very long. In 1875 Rutherford was nominated for another term as Governor, edging out Alphonso Taft, the father of future President William Howard Taft. He was once again elected, and once again the family moved to Columbus.

In June of 1876 the Republican National Convention met in Cincinnati to nominate candidates for President and Vice President of the United States. At that time Rutherford B. Hayes was a respected Governor of an important state, and

---

[21] Diary, June 10, 1874.
[22] Diary, November 25, 1874.
[23] Diary, March 18, 1875.
[24] Diary, March 28, 1875.

that some should think of him for the nomination was only natural. He was neither an unknown dark horse nor a frontrunner, but rather a legitimate contender available in the wings if called upon. He was supported by the delegates from his own state, but most importantly he was the second choice of many delegates from around the country. If their favorites faltered in the balloting, they would be going to their second preference.

Some were not waiting for a call from the wings, however. Congressman James A. Garfield and Senator John Sherman, both of Ohio, were buttonholing everyone they could to line up support for Rutherford. Webb Hayes, astute young political assistant that he was, spoke with anyone who would listen about the merits of his father. Representative James G. Blaine of Maine was the frontrunner, but he could not muster the necessary majority vote for the nomination. Webb sent a message to his father that "if Blaine is not nominated on the 4th ballot your nomination is considered to be certain."[25]

During this time of excitement at the convention Lucy was at home in the Governor's mansion in Columbus. Undoubtedly she was thrilled by the possibility of Rutherford being nominated and being elected President, and with the possibility of the whole family moving to the White House. Whose blood would not race at such prospects?

Blaine's weakness as a candidate was precisely where Rutherford was strong - personal honesty and integrity. In an era torn by political corruption and a scandalous Grant Administration, people wanted someone with a completely clean slate. If Rutherford was anything, it was honest. Blaine, however, had his own personal scandals, and they dragged him down. On the first ballot, Blaine led with 285 votes, followed by Hayes in fifth place with 61 votes from nine states. From there Blaine moved further ahead but always fell short of a majority of the delegates. Just as Webb predicted, Blaine failed on the fourth ballot and Rutherford was nominated on the seventh.

"I must make it my constant effort to deserve this confidence," he wrote humbly.[26] When the Democratic Party met in July and nominated Governor Samuel J. Tilden of New York, it was felt that the election would be very close, with New York, New Jersey, and Connecticut now doubtful for the Republicans. In the tradition of the nineteenth century, Hayes did not campaign, but rather let surrogates go around the country speaking for him and arranging to get out the votes. He claimed in his diary that he was strangely indifferent to the outcome of the election.[27]

---

[25] Doug Wead, *All the President's Children*, New York: Atria Books, 2003, p. 187.
[26] Diary, June 23, 1876.
[27] Diary, November 5, 1876.

Lucy had only a short time to celebrate Rutherford's nomination. Immediately afterward Birchard, who was then twenty three years old, came down with a severe case of typhoid fever. She spent four weeks nursing him back to health. Lucy well knew that children did not always recover from afflictions, but fortunately, in this case, he did.

Finally, though, the personal pride in her husband and the thrill of the election before them did come through to Lucy. They made a trip to Pennsylvania for the Ohio Day observance of the Philadelphia Centennial Exposition. They were tumultuously greeted by thousands of people. "It was one of the happiest days in your mother's life," Lucy wrote to her son Rud. "The enthusiasm of the people, the expressions of pleasure and joy at your father's appearance, touched the old wife who has known his merits for many years." She went on to say that "altogether his past year has been a very bright one in our lives." With the election just days away, the expected closeness of the contest made her thoughtful. "[I]f we are defeated we can personally bear it well, but then comes the thought of our beloved country... Well, we must do our utmost for the right and then leave it to...Providence."[28]

Lucy herself became the subject of many newspaper articles throughout the country. There was a natural public interest in who might become the White House hostess, what kind of person she was. This was the beginning of a life before the public which would continue for the remainder of her days.

On election night, November 7, 1876, the results came in from around the country by telegraph. "Then came, one at a time, towns and precincts in Ohio.... [S]oon we began to feel that Ohio was not doing as well as we had hoped. The effect was depressing. I commanded without much effort my usual composure and cheerfulness. Lucy felt it more keenly. Without showing it [her depression], she busied herself about refreshments for our guests, and soon disappeared. I found her soon after abed with a headache. I comforted her by consoling talk; she was cheerful and resigned, but did not return to the parlor.... I went to bed at 12 to 1 o'clock. Talked with Lucy, consoling her with such topics as readily occurred of a nature to make us feel satisfied on merely personal grounds with the result. We soon fell into a refreshing sleep and the affair seemed over."[29]

As we have seen in the opening chapter of this book, the affair was not over. Rutherford and Lucy Hayes were headed for the White House.

---

[28] Letter Lucy to son Rutherford, dated November 2, 1877, Papers.
[29] Diary, November 11, 1877.

Chapter 6

THE FIRST LADY

When she became the First Lady of the United States on March 5, 1877, Lucy Hayes was ready for the job. As her friend Elizabeth Rust pointed out years later, "she had been the wife of the Governor of Ohio for three terms. She was in the full maturity of middle life, a close observer, a keen and incisive judge of character and motives. She had beauty, grace and dignity. She had such tact that she was sure to be mistress of the situation, however difficult. But, best of all, she had an exacting conscience, quick sympathies, an unselfish nature, and that rare common sense which kept her steady and unspoiled."[1]

This is a fair assessment of Lucy Hayes, but she possessed other characteristics not on the list. She was firm he in her religion, and she and Rutherford lived it, not to the liking of society at large but to suit their own beliefs. Lucy was educated and politically informed, but she was not the activist hoped for by the feminists of the era. She was, without regret, a woman of her own times. She always remembered that it was her husband, and not she, who had been elected President of the United States. She would use her tenure as First Lady as an opportunity to provide a moral example to the country. The upcoming years at the White House were an adventure and an honor, but in the final analysis Lucy knew that this was only a temporary diversion amidst a lifetime of self improvement, husband, children, friends and doing good for others.

The considerable structure called the White House serves a twofold purpose. It is the office space of the President where he works and conducts the business of government, and it is the home of the President's family. Like any other family that moves into a new residence, the Hayes had to make this house their home.

---

[1] Mrs. R. S. Rust, *Lucy Webb Hayes: A Memorial Sketch*, Cincinnati, Cranston & Stowe, 1890, p. 27.

They knew they would be there for only four years, but they intended to fully make it their own during that time.

When they moved into the presidential mansion, the family consisted of Rutherford and Lucy, and their youngest children, nine year old Fanny and six year old Scott. Webb, just graduated from Cornell University, had the great good luck to come home to serve as his father's personal secretary, so he also lived in the White House.

Away from home at this time were Birchard and Rud. They remained at Harvard and Cornell to continue their studies, and came to the White House only occasionally. When they did visit, they sometimes found themselves without a room of their own. These two sons shunned the fame and attention of being in the First Family, and went ahead with their lives as if their parents were living back in Spiegel Grove. They were present, however, for the inauguration and the opening days in the White House.

In addition to this nucleus, the extended Hayes and Webb families and numerous friends from Ohio were always welcome guests. They were always coming and going. Rutherford's niece, Emily Platt, and Emma Foote and Lucy Cook were single young women often visiting for lengthy periods of time. In its totality, it was a bustling household that would more than fill the private quarters of the White House.

Webb Hayes served as his father's "unofficial" but actual personal secretary throughout the term of office. He was with the President almost the entire day, working with him in the office during the day and living in the family quarters afterward. He had earlier served this same function when his father was Governor. There was an added dimension in that he was now also his father's bodyguard, and he always carried a pistol with him. Abraham Lincoln's assassination a dozen years earlier was fresh in everyone's mind, and there were threats received, so this was a vital role. Webb stood next to the President in receiving lines, and accompanied him almost wherever he went. He also had the pleasurable assignment of escorting single young ladies who were invited to various events at the White House.

Fanny was "the pet of the White House" according to staff member William H. Crook. "She was attractive, with a perfect complexion and a bright face." She would go into Crook's office and ask for paper, then sit and write him a note. One note said "private" on the outside, with Fanny's notation in a corner, "very bad writing." She was just like her mother in saying such a thing. Inside, the note said, "Dear Sir, I thank you very much for the paper you gave me. Fanny." Another one said she was "very very very mad" because Crook did not have a book big enough to press flowers in. Still another note said Crook should pay a debt Fanny heard he owed, and was signed, "F. R. Hayes."[2] On a visit to a Methodist Fair in Baltimore in February of 1878 a carpenter presented the President and Lucy with a three storey Victorian doll house for Fanny, which thereafter was actively used by her and prominently displayed in the White House family quarters.[3]

Tutors were arranged for the Fanny and Scott, who had lessons in an improvised school in the mansion. It was located in the historic room from which Lincoln had addressed the crowds below a few years earlier. Later, Lucy wrote a letter thanking a Miss Peyton for the pleasant and happy school days in which she had taught her children.

In making the White House their own home, the Hayes family brought in their own animals. Scott had a goat and a couple of dogs. Lucy had a mockingbird, and soon received a gift of a Siamese cat from the U.S. Consul in Bangkok. She named it "Siam," and it was free to wander through the house. Whenever Lucy entered a room to greet someone, the cat was often making his own entrance at the same time. Late in 1879, while Rutherford and Lucy were away on a visit to Ohio, the cat became sick and the best efforts of the White House physician could not save it.[4] Lucy had a brand new Bradbury upright piano placed in the private parlor of the house, which she played herself on frequent occasions and found it to be an excellent musical instrument.[5]

On his 55th birthday on October 4, 1877, Rutherford reflected upon his family as it was at that time. It is interesting to note his focus on personal qualities rather than worldly achievements, something that Lucy would surely have agreed with. "My family affairs are satisfactory," he wrote. There was no mention of the occupations, homes or social status of any of them. "The three grown boys are truthful, honest, moral, and gentlemanly. Birchard is conscientious, scholarly, but not so practical yet as I hope he will become. Webb is full of sense of the practical sort. Ruddy not yet quite equal to the others, but improving, and is like both. Fanny, now ten years old, is very sensible, does not take jokes, defends her absent friends, is like Mother Hayes. Scott is a handsome little fellow of six - seven in February."

The heart of the husband of Lucy Hayes was also revealed in his dairy that day. "I must resolve on this birthday to do better in the future than ever before," he wrote. "With good health and great opportunities, may I not hope to confer

---

[2] William H. Crook, "Rutherford B. Hayes in the White House" in *The Century Magazine*, March 1909, Volume 77, No. 5, p. 647.

[3] Kenneth E. Davison, *The Presidency of Rutherford B Hayes*, Westport, Connecticut: Greenwood Press, Inc., 1972, p. 77.

[4] *Ibid.*, p 78.

[5] Letter Lucy to F.G. Smith, April 7, 1877, Papers.

great and lasting benefits on my country? I mean to try. Let me be kind and considerate in treatment of the unfortunate who crowd my doorway, and firm and conscientious in dealing with the tempters."[6] He did not explain what he meant by the word "tempters."

The family ate together most evenings in the private quarters. One time John Wise of Virginia came for an appointment with the President, but when Rutherford appeared he had a napkin in his hand. The President invited the guest to join them for their informal but tardy dinner, which he was reluctant to do but finally agreed to because he realized that if he didn't Rutherford would not re-join the family.[7] Wise found Lucy and the children at the table. After dinner the family would generally have a designated hour together where they would talk, help with studies, read together, and otherwise be an ordinary family.

Beyond the First Family and the guests, the White House was attended by a significant staff of cooks, domestics and landscapers. "The very first official act of President Hayes put all of us of the White House staff at our ease," recalled William Crook many years later. Crook began working at the President's House as a doorman under President Lincoln, and rose to the position of executive clerk and disbursing agent. The staff had been anxiously worried that the new President might fire them in favor of his own people, "but in the case of President Hayes we did not have long to wait. The afternoon of Inauguration Day we were all sitting quietly at our desks, with suspense in the air." President Hayes walked in, Crook rose in courtesy from his desk, and they shook hands. Upon inquiry, Crook explained his duties to the President. "'Well,' he said, 'just continue to perform your duties. You will not be disturbed.' I went home that night feeling that the new President was going to be a good man to work for."[8]

Crook recalled that Hayes also introduced a new concept - recording everything that went on at the White House. He hired a stenographer, who stayed in the office all day, writing down everything that was said. Crook felt that this recording of events elevated the tone off what went on in the office.

The Hayes had about a dozen servants in the White House, and they additionally brought in four black domestic helpers from Ohio. One of these was Winnie Monroe, their household cook, and the daughter of one of the Webb slaves who had been freed many years before. She was paid room and board plus $30 per month by the government, and the Hayes gave her an additional $20 from their own funds. Another was "Aunt Clara," another former slave who had been

---

[6] Diary, October 4, 1877.
[7] John S. Wise, *Recollections of Thirteen Presidents*, Freeport, New York: Books for Libraries Press, 1968, p. 138.
[8] Crook, p. 643.

freed by Maria Webb. Isaiah Lancaster had been Rutherford's valet while he was governor, and now continued his duties. The President also supplemented Lancaster's meager salary. The fourth servant was Winnie's daughter, Mary, whose assignment was to assist Lucy in whatever way she was needed.[9]

Later in the year of 1877 Lucy wrote in a letter to her uncle of the change that had come to the Hayes family. ""Our life is quite different from the quiet days in Fremont," she wrote. "Much more busy and responsible than [while Governor] at Columbus and for me quite pleasant and happy.... We have a beautiful view of the Potomac [River] from the Library and bed room windows." Two months later, with controversy swirling around herself and the President, she cautioned her uncle "don't believe everything you hear."[10]

When the Hayes family attended worship services for the first time after the inauguration, they selected the Foundry Methodist Church, which was considered less fashionable compared with Julia Grant's favorite, the Metropolitan Methodist. This change was probably a conscious decision on their part. Lucy did not want to compete with, or walk in the steps of, her predecessor. The Foundry Church had been attended thirty years before by James and Sarah Polk. When a crowd gathered around the Hayes family after the services someone suggested that a rule of etiquette be implemented that everyone remain in place until after the President and his family leaves. "No, dear," said Lucy. "Here we are all on one level."[11] Thereafter Lucy attended class and the children sometimes sang at Sunday School.

The Hayes family did not change their lifelong religious habits merely because Rutherford was President of the United States. They did what they always did. They began the day with scripture reading at breakfast, ending with a kneeling recitation of the Lord's Prayer. It the evenings they would often sing hymns and have prayer.[12] On Sunday mornings they walked as a family to the nearby Foundry Methodist Church, and on Sunday evenings they invited friends, both personal and official, over for singing hymns.

Vice President William Wheeler, a widower who had no children, was to some extent taken under the wing of the Hayes family. They enjoyed a relationship that was closer than perhaps any other between President and Vice President up to that time. Wheeler especially liked singing hymns, and he was a

---

[9] Seale, p. 497.
[10] Letter Lucy to Uncle J. J. Cook, dated November 16, 1877, and January 9, 1878, Papers.
[11] Eliza Davis, *Lucy Webb Hayes: A Memorial Sketch*, Cincinnati: Woman's Home Missionary Society, 1892, p. 53.
[12] Edmund Fuller and David E. Green, *God in the White House: The Faiths of American Presidents*, New York: Crown Publishers, Inc., 1968, p. 136.

regular attender on Sunday evenings. At various times these guests include Congressman William McKinley, General William T. Sherman, Chief Justice Morrison Waite, and their wives. Secretary of the Interior Carl Schurz was usually at the piano. There were critics of these personal events. Some dismissed the Hayes family as religious simpletons who had failed to keep up with a more sophisticated world.

"Every Thanksgiving Day the President and Mrs. Hayes gave a dinner to the secretaries and clerks and their families, carrying out the true spirit of the day by making it an occasion for the children," remembered William Crook. This included the first Thanksgiving in the White House in 1878. "Dinner was served early in the evening, so that the little ones could come. There were placecards for each and souvenirs for the children. The dinner was as elaborately served as the most ceremonious of state dinners."

"After dinner every one gathered in the Red Parlor, and Mrs. Hayes played games with the children....Fanny and Scott joining in. At last all, about twenty-five in the company, drifted around the piano. Mrs. Hayes played, and we all sang hymns together," Crook said. "I suppose some persons would feel inclined to smile at the simplicity of it all; but not any one who was there."[13]

As mentioned in an earlier chapter, Rutherford and Lucy loved Christmas. This did not stop because they were in the White House. Lucy had a present for every one of the household, including the servants, the secretaries, clerks and door keepers. At noon on Christmas Day every one was called into the library, where they found presents in a heap in the middle of the floor. The President or his wife read out the names of the recipients and Fanny and Scott would distribute them. "It was a real Christmas that came to the White House in those days," said Crook, "and Mrs. Hayes's smile was bigger than egg-nog."[14]

Right after their first Christmas in the White House came Rutherford and Lucy's twenty-fifth wedding anniversary. Family and friends began gathering for the commemoration days beforehand. On the day before they took a tour of George Washington's home, Mount Vernon, across the Potomac River in Virginia. December 30, 1877, was a Sunday so on that day they held only a quiet family gathering that day, but the following day they had a big celebration. Lucy wore her original wedding dress, after having the hems let out. Reverend McCabe, the minister who had performed the wedding, now an old man, was present and made some remarks. Rutherford amd Lucy then renewed their wedding vows, and he presented her with a miniature portrait of himself, set amid diamonds. Letters

---

[13] Crook, pp. 661-663.
[14] Crook, pp. 663-664.

from friends not in attendance were read for the group. There was an excellent dinner, with fancy placecards with names as souvenirs for those present. With all in attendance in a circle around them, Fanny and Scott were baptized christened, as their older brothers had been before them. There was singing. It was great event for the family, fondly remembered by Lucy for the rest of her life.

An immediate challenge that came to Lucy Hayes as First Lady was the failure of Congress to appropriate money for the refurbishing of the White House. It was a customary thing to make a grant for this purpose at the beginning of each new administration, but the angry Democratic Congress extended this discourtesy to the Republican President because of the conviction that the presidency had been stolen. It was a petty thing.

This did not stop the needed improvement project, however. Lucy personally administered the task of freshening the walls, carpets, drapes, and furniture. She had everything inventoried, including stored items, which created the first comprehensive listing of White House furnishings. In the end she very frugally restored the appearance of the President's House.

"We had to resort to reversing the ends of the curtains, covering worn spots in the carpets with furniture," wrote son Rud about the situation, "and all sorts of subterfuges to keep it in harmony with what is expected of the Chief Executive's mansion."[15] When a new Congress came into office in 1879, it relented and appropriated money for the White House.

Lucy also improved appearances by a huge production of fresh flowers. She loved flowers and loved to give them to others. The White House conservatory had never been of significant size or importance, but Lucy soon changed that. She had them greatly expanded and growing a vast array of flowers and plants. She brought florist Henry Pfister from Ohio to manage the operation. The billiard room was converted to the cultivation of flowers.

"A rose house and a violet house were constructed and long-closed windows were opened that guests seated at a state dinner could look through long vistas in the conservatory," recalled William Crook years later. Lucy gave flowers away to the Children's Hospital, sick friends and staff. When she was away on a trip to New York in May of 1878 to visit the home of Vice President Wheeler, she wrote back to Rutherford to have flowers sent to the Children's Hospital twice a week. "Her love for flowers was as distinctive as her dress," said Crook. She liked to wear white camellias on her dress and in her hair.[16]

---

[15] Margaret Harrington, "An Abstract of Lucy Webb Hayes as First Lady of the United States," Master thesis, Bowling Green State University, Bowling Green, Ohio, 1956, p. 15.

[16] Crook, p. 646.

Crook noted years later that "[d]uring the four years that Mrs. Hayes held social sway, she was never influenced to change in any detail her manner of dressing her hair." All her life she had her hair sharply parted in the middle and pulled to the sides, with a bun in a comb at the back. She never changed that style. Her clothes were similarly conservative. Her dresses were of a heavy material, long sleeved, and high necked. Any "v" or open space below the neckline was covered with a lighter material. She wore no jewelry beyond a silver comb in her hair and sometimes a cameo portrait of Rutherford, set in diamonds, which was from her 25th wedding anniversary.

Editor Alexander K. McClure of the *Philadelphia Times*, a critic of the Washington social scene and its fashionable excesses, very much appreciate the modest example of Lucy Hayes before the nation. He wrote that "Mrs. Hayes deserves the thanks of every true woman for the stand which she has taken against extravagance in dress. She has carried to the White House the same quiet dignity and lady-like simplicity for which she was distinguished at home; and her dress on public occasions, while invariably handsome and becoming the wife of the President, has also been invariably unostentatious."[17]

Of course, Lucy was a keen observer of the political scene, now more than ever. The presidential administration of Rutherford B. Hayes began in a bitter political environment. He had no mandate from the vote of the people, and the opposition in Congress was such that it was nearly impossible to move ahead with any kind of national agenda. Had Rutherford run for a second term and won a clear majority of the popular vote and the electoral college, things might have been different in a second term, but he, like James K. Polk before him, had said from the outset that he would serve only one term. Also like Polk, he kept that promise, and in the end he was glad to do so.

There was a widespread belief that Lucy carried great weight with Rutherford on all matters, including political policy. When Lucy left Washington for a period of time one newspaper wrote that "Mr. Hayes will, during the absence of Mrs. Hayes, be acting President."[18] Rutherford substantiated this somewhat when he wrote that, "I don't know how much influence Mrs. Hayes has with Congress, but she has great influence with me."[19] Yet the truth of it is that Lucy rarely sought to exercise any political influence with her husband.

People and conditions are always changing. Nothing in this country has remained the same for very long, and it was as true in the nineteenth century as it

---

[17] Paul F. Boller, Jr., *Presidential Wives: An Anecdotal History*, New York: Oxford University Press, 1988, pp. 147-148.
[18] Anthony, p. 231.
[19] *Ibid*

is now. In the 1870s women were beginning to have new opportunities opened to them than had been the case in the past. While most women fulfilled traditional roles, some, like Lucy Webb, were getting more education than ever before. Working opportunities opened in offices and factories. Women became the key support of social reform movements for temperance laws to restrict alcohol, child labor laws to prevent exploitation of minors, voting rights for women, and greater education for all. The term "New Woman" gain common usage as a description of the women who supported these goals, and as a name for the idea woman they sought to create in society.

Many people in 1877 looked to the well educated and articulate First Lady as the rising example of the New Woman, and to be the symbol of the movement. Lucy Hayes was in fact an example, showing by her own life and way of living the values she thought important. This included some aspects of being a New Woman - being educated, politically informed, and generally enlightened in attitude. But this was not what many people wanted. They didn't really want an example, they wanted an activist. They hoped that Lucy would become the visible spokeswoman of the cause, a leader of the reforms they supported. In this hope they would be very disappointed.

Lucy Hayes was intent on being, and inwardly content to be, herself. She was not interested in being a New Woman activist. She would remain who and what she was before becoming First Lady, and, like all her predecessors, she would not use her position as wife of the President as a means to advance her personal causes. It is different now in an era of politically active First Ladies, but Lucy Hayes must be seen in the context in which she lived. No one ever recorded that Rutherford kept Lucy politically repressed or isolated, or that Lucy was frustrated and angry over an inability to crusade for the political causes of her choosing.

Margaret Truman, the daughter of President Harry Truman, in her own book on First Ladies wrote that "[t]o the consternation of these true believers, in her four years in the White House...Lucy did not say a single word on behalf of women reformers... Why? Because woman's rights was an extremely unpopular issue in the late eighteen seventies, and Lucy Hayes was first, last, and always a politician's wife.... Politician's wives live in the present, not some theoretical future, and Lucy Hayes was acutely aware that her husband was in no position to tolerate a controversial wife."[20]

This characterization is overly cynical. Rutherford announced from the beginning that he would serve only one term of office, and he and Lucy were free to be themselves without fear of losing re-election. It is true that Lucy well played

---

[20] Margaret Truman, *First Ladies,* New York: Random House, 1995, p. 49.

the role of a politician's wife, but it is also true that she did not want to actively advance any causes. She did what she wanted, and these causes - before, during and after the presidency - were at the fringes of her life. Margaret Truman need look further than her own mother, Bess, for an example of a First Lady who honorably had no interest in being the poster child for anyone's cause. Bess and Lucy were both determined to be themselves while First Lady, and they ignored the expectations of others.

There was one social cause, the temperance movement, in which Lucy deeply believed. All her life she followed the principles it espoused but was not activist as her grandfather had been. Nevertheless, just being herself got her into a great deal of political controversy.

Rutherford and Lucy Hayes had long ago decided as a couple that they were against alcohol and that they would not serve it in their home. This did not change when they moved into their new home in Washington, D.C. Although the White House is the working office of the Chief Executive, it is also the residence of the President and his family, and they have the right to set the rules of what happens in their own home. This is just what they did. Alcohol would not be served in their home. Their friend Eliza Davis said they decided it together before the ever took the train to Washington in February.

Unfortunately, there was an initial stumble on the issue. As soon as they were in the White House they were faced with the official state visit of the adult sons of Czar Alexander II, the Russian grand dukes Alexis and Constantine. They were making a grand tour of the United States, and were scheduled to be at the first state dinner of the Hayes Administration, on April 17, 1877. When the subject of whether to serve wine at the dinner came up, Secretary of State William M. Evarts said it would be a slight to the Russian nation not to serve it. So it was served.

It is apparent that Rutherford and Lucy were not happy with themselves over having permitted this to happen. In their own home they had allowed something which they very much opposed. It was decided that it would not happened again. Alcohol was thenceforth banned in the White House.

It is not clear now whether Rutherford made the decision and Lucy merely implemented it, or whether Lucy convinced her husband, who went along with his wife's wishes. Statements from contemporaries and historians go both ways. It seems likely that it was a decision in which they both concurred. Neither were prohibitionists, and they did not seek to impose their will on others. Their fundamental feeling was that this their home and what went on there was their own personal business

It caused a national uproar. Newspaper editorials and cartoons ridiculed them as religious zealots, as bigots intent on controlling the conduct of others, and as simple fools. "Because of the attitude of President Mrs. Hayes toward the temperance movement, a large element of the country thought them narrow-minded fanatics. But there was nothing fanatical about them," said White House staff member William Crook. "Beyond the one instance of the stand with regard to their own table at the White House, they made no effort to interfere in the affairs of others. They could be genial and companionable without being untrue to their principles. They were hospitable and loved to put their best before friends. Although he President did not smoke there was rarely a time when they did not have cigars for their guests."[21]

In the final analysis, of course, Rutherford was the President and he had to own the decision. Some accused him of a political motive, of wanting to keep the supporters of the temperance movement within the Republican Party rather than going over to the newly formed Prohibition Party. In light of the history of Rutherford and Lucy banning liquor in their own home, it seems unfair to say that now in the White House they were acting for purely political reasons.

Even though Rutherford had the final decision, Lucy caught the blame from the many critics. Gossip, jokes, political cartoons and mean spirited remarks were everywhere. One joke was that "water flowed like wine." Some felt that to impose the liquor ban on others was wrong, particularly upon foreign dignitaries. She was tagged with the nickname "Lemonade Lucy," which through history has been said with a derogatory or admiring implication, depending upon the antagonism or support of the speaker. Rutherford and Lucy stayed the course, however. This was their house and they would manage it. If others wanted to follow their example, they would surely have been pleased.

Many people throughout the country supported the decision, and were proud of the President and his wife. Frances E. Willard, the president of the Women's Christian Temperance Union (WCTU) actively sought to bring Lucy within their cause. Lucy, however, would not be brought. Shortly after the inauguration a minister's wife asked Lucy not to serve alcohol at the White House. "Madam, it is my husband, not myself, who is President," the First Lady curtly responded. "I think a man who is capable of filling so important a position as I believe my husband to be, is quite competent of establishing such rules as will occur in his house without calling on members of other households."[22] Lucy would not be an activist, nor interfere in political matters.

Their decision was for themselves only; they did not wish to impose it upon others. This was proven in 1878 when Lucy dropped a comment while on a trip to

---

[21] Crook, pp. 656-657.
[22] Eckenrode, p. 230.

New York which left some supporters aghast. "I do not use wine or liquors myself nor in my family, but I have no thought of shunning those who think or act differently," she said. "It is a mistake to think that I should want to be so dictatorial. I want people to enjoy themselves in the manner that is the most pleasing to them." This was too much for those who wanted to ban liquor altogether.

Now she was blasted from the other side, the prohibitionists. The members of the Lucy Hayes Temperance Society in Washington, which had adopted her name without her consent in expectation of her support for the cause, were furious. They adopted a very angry and harsh resolution concluding with the statement: "Be it resolved, that this society discards the name of Mrs. R. B. Hayes, and pronounces her as complete a fraud as her husband."[23] If Lucy ever read this attack, which she probably did, it had to hurt, despite all her efforts to be politically tough. Hopefully, she also heard that the society president, who was not present when the resolution was adopted, repudiated the intemperate wording of the resolution.

That the decision was for themselves only was also shown on a trip to Richmond in October 1877 to the Virginia State Fair. The Southern Railroad Company furnished a car with meals to the presidential party, and it included alcohol. This railroad car was not their home, and the President and Mrs. Hayes made no objection. Their own glasses, however, remained turned down.[24]

Margaret Truman discussed Lucy Hayes and the no alcohol decision in her book, giving an excellent explanation of the underlying motive for prohibition in the White House. "The liquor ban was not a decision the Hayeses made casually, or on impulse. They knew it was going to cause them trouble. They made it because they feared America of 1877 was in danger of drowning in booze.... [I]n nineteenth century America the number of homes and marriages destroyed by alcohol was astronomical.... Washington, D.C., probably had more heavy drinkers per capita than any other city in the union in those days.... But the President and his wife wanted to send a message to the nation about their opposition to alcohol - a message 1877 America needed as badly as it needed a strong stand against drugs in the nineteen eighties."[25]

History has, on balance, been unkind to Lucy Hayes over this issue. The alliterative "Lemonade Lucy" had a ring to it that has stuck to her for more than a century, almost reducing her entire life to a simple nickname. Within its two

[23] Newspaper *National Republican*, April 27, 1878, Papers.
[24] Crook, pp. 657-658.
[25] Truman, pp. 47-48.

words she is implied to be narrow, self-righteous and meddling. Suffice it to say, she was actually the opposite of these things.

For those who wanted to condemn Lucy for narrow-mindedness, they found comfort in a rumor making the rounds late in the administration. A pioneer of women seeking ordination as a minister in the Methodist Episcopal Church, the Reverend Mrs. Anna Oliver delivered a sermon she entitled, "Lessons from the life of Lucy Webb Hayes." Rutherford said it was "excellent," so it must have been complimentary. In that talk , however, she unknowingly passed along a rumor which was untrue, that Lucy had intervened to stop a card game between Cabinet members and the President. It was intended as a compliment. It was repeated by many as a criticism, an illustration of intolerance by the First Lady. In reality there was nothing to ban because the activity was not one that anyone engaged in. "No such occurrence took place," said Rutherford. "It is true there was no card playing at the White House by Cabinet officers or others with the President or Mrs. Hayes as neither of them play cards. But the anecdote in question was a pure invention, told by a correspondent as a joke."[26]

Lucy Hayes was criticized for taking a stand on alcohol in the White House, and for not taking a stand on other political issues. At that time the Constitution of the United States said nothing about whether women should or should not vote. It was a state issue, and some states were moving in the direction of having women vote. This was particularly true in the Western states, where the territorial legislatures of Wyoming in 1869 and Utah in 1870 became the first to endorse it. The movement was growing, but still very far from achieving its goal of full voting rights for women.

Women suffragists hoped that the First Lady would support their cause, but she refused to do so. Rutherford at one point wrote in his diary that when it came to female voting, "My point...is that the proper discharge of the function of maternity is inconsistent with the like discharge of the duties of citizenship."[27] So far as is known, Lucy never challenged him on this subject, publicly or privately. When political activists Susan B. Anthony and Elizabeth Cady Stanton came to the White House to meet with the President on the issue of women's suffrage, Lucy did not attend. She came in only at the end of the meeting to give the ladies a tour of the mansion.[28]

Lucy was the first wife of a President to have graduated from college, but she did not openly support the cause of education for girls and women. At that time less than one per cent of all women 18 to 21 went to college. In 1878 she was

---

[26] Diary, August 25, 1881.
[27] Diary, April 27, 1870.
[28] Betty Boyd Caroli, *First Ladies*, New York: Oxford University Press, 1987, p. 93.

invited by Rachel L. Bodley, a fellow student in earlier days back in Ohio, to attend the commencement at the Women's Medical College of Philadelphia. The purpose of the visit was to make a show of support for the professional education of women. Lucy declined the invitation. Sometime later she did go there but in the company of Rutherford, and he spoke, not she. When Congress was considering a bill to allow women lawyers to appear and argue cases before the United States Supreme Court, Susan B. Anthony and Elizabeth Cady Stanton asked Lucy to encourage her husband to support it. She declined to do so.[29]

Another issue upon which Lucy remained silent was that of equal wages for women. As early as 1854 Lucy and Rutherford's sister, Fanny, had attended a speech by Lucy Stone. The speaker was an abolitionist and early women's rights advocate who toured the country speaking on behalf of these causes. After listening to her presentation, Lucy told Rutherford at the time that she supported better wages for women, and could understand the use of violence to get attention focused of the issue.[30] Now, as First Lady, she probably still felt the same way, but did not use her position to advance the cause. This was all very frustrating to the advocates of these causes.

Throughout the administration the President and Mrs. Hayes had an active and ongoing social calendar, entertaining often and generously. When asked if all of it was tiring, Lucy said, "Why, I never get tired of having a good time."[31] In public receptions Lucy would stand beside Rutherford, both shaking the hands of hundreds of people, non-stop sometimes for hours. Her gloves would become soiled as the night progressed. They ended the tradition of permitting walk-ins into evening receptions, and for the first time instituted a new tradition of invitations. These written invitations became highly prized keepsakes for those who received them.

Lucy, without her husband, held regular Saturday afternoon public receptions in the Blue Parlor, and during the social season of the winter months had them on many weekday afternoons. At these events she always had the wife of a Cabinet member stand beside her in the reception line. She was careful not to offend the wives. At her first reception she had all Cabinet wives with her in the receiving line. Thereafter she had one Cabinet wife with her, then all of them again at the last event and the end of the administration.

"Mrs. Hayes always had a fondness for girls. She loved to surround herself with you and pretty faces. There were always young women guests at the White House, sometimes relatives, sometimes friends or the daughters of old friends,"

---

[29] Boller, p. 151.
[30] Boller, p. 150.
[31] Crook, p. 658.

recalled William Crook many years later. "The number of luncheons for women, young and old, and the lovely spirit of sunny friendliness prevalent at them, made Mrs. Hayes' reign one long to be remembered."[32]

When formal state dinners were coming, Lucy would personally take charge of the preparations. Days beforehand she would give instructions to the staff as to decorations, music, ushers and catering. Then she supervised as it was all brought together for the appointed hour.[33] Over the four years they had hundreds of dinner guests, including future Presidents James A. Garfield and William McKinley, many relatives and family friends, numerous generals including George Crook and Manning Force for whom two of their sons were named, members of the Cabinet, the Senate, the Supreme Court and the House of Representatives, diplomats and many others. When President Ulysses S. Grant and Julia Grant returned from their trip around the world they were invited to dine at their old residence.

"It is very gratifying to see the heartiness and warmth of friendship for Lucy," Rutherford wrote in his diary in May 1879. "Her large warm heart and lively sympathy for or with all around her, with a fair share of beauty and talents, have made her wonderfully popular."[34]

In the spring of 1878 Lucy began a tradition which still is followed today. She opened up the South Lawn of the White House grounds for neighborhood children to come and engage in an "Easter egg roll" on the Monday after Easter. This consisted of the children rolling a brightly decorated egg down the grassy hillside in an effort to go the furthest without breaking it. The hiding of eggs and the hunt for them also was involved. Lucy thought of this as a wholesome activity that the entire family could enjoy. First Lady Dolley Madison had been the hostess for such an event on the grounds of the Capitol Building, but when Congress made its site unavailable Lucy moved it to the White House. Next to the fame of "Lemonade Lucy," this is the second most famous remembrance of Lucy's years as First Lady.

In all of her social interaction Lucy went to great pains not to offend anyone, but there was one person with whom she had an open breach. This was the wife of James G. Blaine. Blaine had lost the 1876 Republican presidential nomination to Rutherford, and his wife, Harriet, was still angry about it. She apparently felt that she, and not Lucy, should be the First Lady. "For no reason in the world except perhaps that Mr. Hayes and not Mr. Blaine had reached the White House in 1877, Mrs. Blaine began a system of persecutions as soon as Mrs. Hayes came to

---

[32] Crook, p. 661.
[33] Kathleen Prindiville, *First Ladies*, New York: The Macmillan Company, 1954, p. 165.
[34] Diary, May 28, 1879.

Washington," Hayes family friend Thomas C. Donaldson wrote later. In a gesture of reconciliation, the Blaines were invited to a White House dinner on January 29, 1878. It didn't go well. Harriet did not eat a thing during the entire meal. This was noticed by all and sent Washington society to twittering. It was rumored that she told someone afterward that the table was so crowded she could not lift her arm, and that she told another that she would never eat in the White House so long as Hayes was there. She was never given the opportunity again.

The ill will continued. While in New York City Lucy and her son Rud were at a restaurant table when Mrs. Blaine entered at the door. She headed straight for the table, but then veered off and sat at another. At a musical in Washington Lucy and a friend unknowingly sat next to Mrs. Blaine, who promptly picked up her belongings and moved to another seat. Seeing what was going on, Lucy said to her companion in a loud stage whisper, "Bettie, who was that stout old person in purple?" Lucy was not sorry to see Blaine lose the nomination again in 1880 to her friend James A. Garfield.

"She never seems to forget a slight nor fail to reward a friend," Donaldson concluded. "She is brainy, brave and discreet, with any amount of nerve.... A good friend, a dangerous enemy, and withal a loving and charitable woman."[35]

In the hot and humid months of summer, Washington, D.C., without air conditioning was an uncomfortable place to be. Congress had historically adjourned for the summer and fled to cooler places. Presidents did their best to find ways to either leave town or find the best accommodations possible. In the days before Camp David, the Maryland haven of modern presidents, it was popular to go to the National Soldier's Home just outside Washington. This is what the Hayes family did each summer. A great deal of furniture would be taken there in June, then back to the White House in October.

The family lived in what was called the Anderson Cottage. Lincoln had stayed there, but not Johnson or Grant. It was an inviting structure conducive to outdoor summer living, with porches with rocking chairs looking out over shady trees and inviting lawns and porches. "We find life at the Soldier's Home very pleasant," Lucy wrote in August of 1880.[36]

Rutherford and Lucy traveled around the country more than any previous presidential couple. They went on trips back home to Ohio, together and separately, and to Boston and much of New England for Birchard's graduation from Harvard. Maryland, Pennsylvania and Virginia were within a very short distance and they visited often. In May of 1878 Lucy went with Vice President

---

[35] "The Memoirs of Thomas C. Donaldson," *Hayes Historical Journal*, 1979, p. 146, Rutherford B. Hayes Presidential Center Library.
[36] Letter Lucy to Mr. Laurence, dated August 29, 1880, Papers.

Wheeler to visit his home area of New York, where they went fishing in the Adirondack Mountains. Wheeler wired back that Lucy had caught a fifteen pound salmon, which was iced and shipped back to the White House where Rutherford invited friends over for a fish dinner.[37]

This trip occurred amidst the seemingly endless political controversy that comes with being President of the United States. "Sometimes I feel a little worried as I think of you all alone and this press and annoyance going on ," Lucy wrote back to Rutherford on June 4th, "but I keep myself outwardly very quiet and calm, but inwardly (sometimes) there is a burning venom and wrath - all under a smiling or pleasant exterior."[38] She was soon feeling better, however. After receiving many kind acts by women she encountered, Lucy wrote the President that "how much happier I am with my disposition of confidence than if I doubted and sought for the selfish reason of acts."[39] She preferred to accept a kindness at face value and look no further for motives..

In the late summer of 1880 they went on the first presidential trip to the American West. This took the President of the United States away from the Washington for seventy two days, something never done before and which could never be done in modern circumstances. They departed on August 26th and did not return to Washington, D.C., until November 6th. On September 5th they arrived in Salt Lake City in the Utah Territory, and were welcomed by Mormon Church President John Taylor. Lucy met with Latter Day Saint women leaders, then went with her husband to Methodist services in the evening.[40]

From there they went northward to Vancouver and Seattle in the Washington Territory, Portland, Oregon, and San Francisco and Los Angeles in California. No sitting President had ever been to the West Coast before, and they were warmly greeted by large crowds wherever they went. Lucy wrote back to Fanny to have Webb point out on a map to Fanny and Scott where their parents were visiting.

Heading eastward from Los Angeles, they crossed Arizona, which still was endangered by Indian war parties, by train until the tracks ran out in New Mexico. When the tracks ran out they took a three days journey in a carriage. After attending a fiesta in Santa Fe, they continued by train and continued homeward. On November 1, 1880, they reached Spiegel Grove, and then went back to the political and social whirlwind that was Washington.

---

[37] Diary of Webb Hayes, File Folders, Rutherford B. Hayes Presidential Center Library.
[38] Letter Lucy to Rutherford, dated June 4, 1878, Papers.
[39] Letter Lucy to Rutherford, dated August 11, 1878, Papers.
[40] "Lemonade Lucy and the Anti-Polygamy Crusade: First Lady Lucy Webb Hayes as Symbol" by Patricia Lynn Scott, 1998, manuscript in the File Folders, Rutherford B. Hayes Presidential Center Library.

Throughout the White House years Lucy continued her mothering of Birchard and Rud by mail. In a letter to Rud she said she was glad to hear he was having a good time, but cautioned him to be careful of his conduct, and to think of what his mother would think of whatever he was doing.[41] She wrote to Birch that "I have a great deal of faith in an over ruling Providence to guide us finally aright, and since we have been here my faith has not lessened but increased."[42]

Modern inventions were coming fast during the 1870s, and some of them were demonstrated for the First Family. In April of 1878 the young inventor Thomas Edison brought over one of his new phonographs to the White House, and the fascinated President and First Lady stayed up until 3:30 a.m. enjoying the new contraption. Alexander Graham Bell demonstrated the telephone and one was installed in the White House on a trial basis in May of 1879 by the National Telephone Company. Unfortunately, it was of little use because very few others had phones to call. Typewriters, which came on to the commercial market in the 1870s, were brought in for the clerks on February 12, 1880. Unlike the telephone, they were of immediate practical use.[43]

An unhappy aspect of Lucy's fame was the exploitation of her image by commercial marketers. They shamelessly, and without permission, used the likeness of the First Lady on products and in magazines. Her face was seen by the people regularly on newsstands and in markets and dry goods stores. It made her one of the most famous and recognizable people in the country.

As an educated woman, knowledgeable in history and politics, she treasured the experience of being in the famed White House. There was talk at that time about building a new mansion, perhaps having the President's office in one building and his family living in another one. When asked by a reporter writing under the pen name of "Miss Grundy" whether she would like to have a new house for the President's family, Lucy said no. "I would not wish to exchange this [house] for any other. I think it beautiful," she said. "I love this house for the associations that no other could have,"[44] She was, of course, right. No other place of any description could match the history of the White House.

Lucy wanted to enhance the historical mansion by creating a collection of images of the Presidents and their wives who had preceded her there. At the time there was no central depository of such artwork. She actively sought the purchase a full length (then) modern painting of Martha Washington to provide a match with an older work of President George Washington. Congress ultimately

---

[41] Letter Lucy to son Rutherford, January 31, 1879, Papers.
[42] Letter Lucy to son Birchard, March 26, 1879, Papers.
[43] Seale, pp. 494-495.
[44] Art for the President's House - An Historical Perspective," The White House Website.

complied with this request, spending the large sum of $3,000 to obtain it. That particular portrait was panned by critics then and now, depicting Martha in an 1870s dress beside an 1870s style chair, but getting *something* into the collection was Lucy's main achievement at the time. Long afterward a more historically accurate depiction of Martha would be obtained, and the portrait obtained by Lucy was relegated to a secondary room.

Lucy embarked on a campaign to acquire images of all of the occupants of the White House. In the 1850s Congress had commissioned artist George P. A. Healy to make images of the presidents then still living, and he did excellent work in fulfilling that assignment, but portraits of earlier presidents, and all of their wives, were lacking. Lucy consulted with the Librarian of Congress, Ainsworth R. Spofford, who at her urging attempted to acquire original Gilbert Stuart portraits of John Adams and Thomas Jefferson from their families. This effort was unsuccessful, so copies were made by the copyist Edgar Parker.

Eliphalet Frazer Andrews of the Corcoran School of Art, who had created the Martha Washington portrait, proposed to the President and Lucy that he research and produce historically credible portraits of other presidents. Julia Gardiner Tyler, widow of President John Tyler, presented a portrait of herself , which became the first portrait of a First Lady to hang in the White House. Lucy invited the ex-Confederate Julia to stand with her in a reception in February of 1878. It is now considered that some of the work Lucy obtained was not first rate, but it was the beginning of a First Ladies collection that grew from her starting point.

Lucy was the first First Lady to have her portrait made for the specific purpose of being placed in a White House collection of artwork of presidents and wives. She selected the nationally renowned Daniel Huntington of the National Academy of Design to do the work, which he completed just prior to the end of the administration. He also made a portrait of Rutherford, which was added to the collection.

It is interesting that Lucy did not like the portrait. "The picture or portrait annoys me," she wrote to Webb.[45] She was also annoyed that the Women's Christian Temperance Union, which offered to pay for it, had difficulty raising the funds. With respect to the fund raising solicitations, Lucy wrote that "this begging is painful to me."[46]

In April of 1880, as the next presidential contest loomed, Rutherford considered in his diary the successes of his administration. Any success was difficult under the circumstances in which his presidency began. Of the twenty

---

[45] Letter Lucy to Webb, dated November 20, 1880, Papers.
[46] Letter Lucy to WCTU, dated 1880, Papers.

points he briefly enumerated, some flowed from the type of people that he and Lucy were, from the manner of personal living that the two of them had chosen over a lifetime. Lucy had as much a part of Rutherford's high standards as he did. These areas of administration success which Rutherford mentioned were the selection of Cabinet officers who were free from personal scandal, a refusal to appoint their own relatives to political offices, and "good morals in the White House."[47]

During the last year of the presidential term, Lucy was increasingly thinking of going home, and looking forward to it. "I have had a happy life," she wrote of the White House to a friend, "and now that it is almost over I look forward with delight to the old home" at Spiegel Grove. Her ever-persistent doubts about her Christian worthiness popped up in the letter. "I am not a good person to be at the head of any active work which requires a known Christian character," she said.[48] Nothing could have been further from reality.

After their return from the West the pace of social activity picked up. The Hayes were leaving and they made the most of their last months. William Crook said dinners in the final months averaged thirty-seven guests. On February 24, 1881, the diplomatic corps in Washington was invited, and all the rooms in the White House, including the conservatories, were used to provide seating for two thousand people.[49]

Two days before the close of the Hayes Administration, the President was reflecting upon the events of the day in his diary. He had received favorable comments from many people, and estimated that he shook hands with five hundred people that day. "Mrs. Hayes seems to be a great and almost universal favorite," he proudly recorded. "Would we were worthier! It is said by old public functionaries and by citizens that no President and his wife and family ever left here so much and so generally regretted."[50]

Staff member William Crook went on to make an assessment of Lucy Hayes personally. "The Hayes family was an affectionate and harmonious one," he said. "To begin with, the President was genial and even-tempered. Mrs. Hayes would have been considered an unusual woman wherever placed. People were always saying she was a clever woman. One would know, from the way she carried herself and from her face, that she was a woman of much character; the deference shown her by her husband would have proved it if nothing else did. But her cleverness was not what most impressed White House employees. What we felt

---

[47] Diary, April 1880.
[48] Letter Lucy to "friend," dated July 22, 1880, Papers.
[49] Gould, p. 227.
[50] Diary, March 2, 1881.

was her sweetness, her kindness, and the sunniness of her disposition. She was a bright, happy woman."[51]

It is unfair to judge the first ladyship of Lucy Hayes through the prism of the twenty-first century. Had she come along in modern times, she undoubtedly would have fulfilled modern expectations. At the end of the Hayes Administration journalist Laura Holloway issued a new edition of her book, entitled "Ladies of the White House." She was the editor of the *Brooklyn Daily Eagle*, and her 1870 book had sold over one hundred thousand copies. She was so favorably impressed with Lucy Hayes that in the new version she divided the first ladies into three categories - the strong women from 1789 to 1829, the weak ones from 1829 to 1877, and a new era beginning with Lucy Hayes. She wrote of Lucy that "[h]er strong healthful influence gives the world assurance of what the next century woman will be."[52]

This statement has since been discounted as being unfulfilled by Lucy's inactions. It was, nonetheless, true. First Lady Lucy Hayes was indeed the forerunner of what twentieth century women would be like - family-oriented, educated and well-read, enlightened in outlook, politically informed, caring of other people, and fulfilling the destiny that she chose for herself. She was a worthy role model for all of these virtues.

As the final day of the administration approached Lucy was looking forward to leaving the White House, the politics, and the presidency behind. "This beautiful morning, after so many dreary wintry days, has filled us all with renewed strength and happiness," she wrote to a friend in January, "and as I entered my room a few moments ago with this glorious sun streaming in and giving everything a glow of happiness." She mentioned with anticipation that Webb was at Spiegel Grove, getting "it ready for the old people to retire to on the 4th of March."[53]

A final White House dinner was held for the extended family on March 2nd. It snowed throughout the night of the 3rd, finally stopping about ten o'clock on the morning of the 4th. Rutherford did some final paperwork, entering a final veto of a Congressional bill. The streets were impassable except for Pennsylvania Avenue, which had been cleared of snow by workmen throughout the night. At about noon , in a cold wind and a freezing temperature, James A. Garfield raised his hand and released Rutherford and Lucy Hayes from their great callings.

After the ceremony Lucy hosted a luncheon for the Garfields, then inspected the White House to make sure all was in order for the new occupants. "All was

---

[51] Crook, p. 644.
[52] Boller, p.150.
[53] Letter Lucy to "dear Major," dated January 1881, Papers.

lovely and serene," she said, "It was well I was so hurried for the goodbyes would have overcome me, for I grew to love the house."[54] That afternoon they sat with the Garfields and watched the traditional inaugural parade down Pennsylvania Avenue, something they had not experienced for themselves. In the evening a reception was held in honor of the outgoing President and First Lady at the home of Secretary of the Treasury John Sherman, where White House staffers and others bade the family farewell.

On the following day Lucy, Rutherford and children were on the train westward to Ohio. About eleven miles out of Washington, at Severn, Maryland, their train was hit by two locomotives going the other direction. Two people were killed, and Lucy for a time consoled the ten year old son of one of the victims. Twenty others were hurt. The Hayes family was shaken but not injured. Leaving the tangle of steel behind, they continued their journey.

The Hayes family reached home in Fremont on the evening of March 8, 1881. The weather was bad but the home town people turned out en masse at the train station to welcome their most famous citizens. Lucy and Rutherford shook a great many hands, and were given an escort in a parade of bands, torches and the general population. Back in Spiegel Grove, they went to bed in their own home.

---

[54] Gould, p. 228.

Chapter 7

RETIREMENT AT SPIEGEL GROVE

When Rutherford and Lucy Hayes took the train back to Ohio in the spring of 1881, they were just 58 and 49 years old. They had every reason to look forward to a long retirement together, but it was not to be. Eight short years were all that fate would allot them.

They always had their eye on returning one day to Spiegel Grove near Fremont, Ohio. As long ago as 1853, shortly after their wedding, the young couple went to Fremont to visit Uncle Birchard. They had a pleasant time, and when Rutherford returned home he wrote to his uncle that "[i]f you don't want any more real estate about Fremont, suppose you look out a bargain or two for me."[1] They went back often. As Uncle Birchard acquired the ground and built the home, Rutherford and Lucy both loved it. "Uncle's new house is large and very handsome, " Rutherford wrote. "Lucy was very much taken with it. I suspect she will prefer it to a city home, after she once gets settled there."[2] Lucy herself said on a visit during the Civil War that "[t]he house is beautiful, so convenient and large. It will be a delightful home if we all live to be united here."[3]

When she visited the place in March of 1880, when the end of the presidency was within view, Lucy wrote to Rutherford that "we will grow old together and lead a happy life at Fremont - the grove looked beautiful and I left with a happy feeling that so soon we would be back again to trees and flowers and the dear old home."[4] Webb went back to Spiegel Grove early, making improvements and expansions and generally getting the place ready for his parents' retirement. They

---

[1] Diary, April 3, 1853, and June 22, 1853.
[2] Diary, December 2, 1859.
[3] Letter Lucy to Rutherford, dated September 7, 1863, Papers.
[4] Letter Lucy to Rutherford, dated March 12, 1880, Papers.

found on their arrival in 1881 that despite Webb's best efforts the preparatory
work on the house was not completed. The front porch had been doubled in size
and a large 26 by 37 foot parlor had been added for Lucy, and the house now had
nine bedrooms. The carpenters and plasterers were still there working, however,
when they arrived.

It was a wooded spot on the outskirts of town in an area of endless flat land,
made beautiful by man's cultivation of trees and farms. Spiegel Grove, meaning
Mirror Grove in German, itself consisted of a large home surrounded by idyllic
grounds. The original house was completely surrounded by a veranda, which
Rutherford loved and used as a walking course in bad weather. Soon, however, he
had the house expanded to about twenty rooms, with ample bedrooms for visitors.
One upstairs room was filled with mementos from the presidential years. Another
room was an excellent library, containing many of the classics that Lucy and
Rutherford loved to read. They liked to spend time there reading and snacking on
home grown apples. The house was equipped with one of the few telephones in
Fremont, and with gas lighting in the parlors.[5] Domestic help included a black
servant woman who maintained the home, a groundskeeper and a coachman who
cared for the horses.

The longtime cook Winnie Monroe had to be discharged from employment
not long after their arrival. Winnie's bad temper was affecting Lucy's good humor
to the point that Lucy decided that it must end. It was a painful thing, as Winnie
had been with them for many years and was loved by the Hayes family. Other
domestic help was brought in.

On August 28, 1881, Rutherford made one of his period accounts of his
family. "Lucy is today fifty years old," he wrote in his diary. " She...enters on her
second half century in good health. We are satisfied with the roominess and
convenience, not to say beauty, of our new home. Our children are healthy and
promising. Birch, a lawyer in Toledo. Webb is a manufacturer of house building
hardware in Cleveland. Rud will spend one year in a scientific school. Fanny,
almost fourteen (September 2), and Scott, ten, will go to school here." With their
two young ones still at home, they were still in the full bloom of parenthood and
raising a family.

Still in his fifties, Rutherford could retire comfortably without the need for
working to support himself and his family. He had a very substantial fortune from
his own labors and from his inheritances from his mother and uncle. He was free
to do, or not do, as he pleased. He worked for various educational and

---

[5] "A Veranda with a House Attached: Life at Spiegel Grove in the Late Nineteenth Century" by Matt
Bloom, Rutherford B. Hayes Presidential Center Library.

philanthropic causes, lending his prestige to several organizations by sitting on their boards of directors, attending conferences and occasionally giving speeches. He sought to improve educational opportunities for black people, and to reform the harsh conditions in prisons.

Lucy was also free to do as she wanted. Her first self-assignment, as always, was to be wife and mother. In the remainder of her time he chose to teach Sunday School, participate in church events such as fairs and dinners, and to accompany her husband on his business trips. She loved to care for the trees, crops and animals they maintained.

They led a very active social life. It is easy to understand that in a small town a former President and First Lady would be on everyone's list for inviting to events. In September they went to the annual reunion of the 23rd Ohio Regiment, something which they frequently did in coming years. Rutherford loved socializing with former comrades in arms and visiting old battlefields, and Lucy loved to be a part of it.

In July of 1881 came the shocking news that Rutherford's successor in the White House, President James A Garfield, had been shot at the train station in Washington. He survived the wound, and struggled to recover for several weeks. Then in September he took a turn for the worse and died. Rutherford returned to Washington to be a part of the official grieving of the nation, and to accompany the body back to Ohio. Lucy met the entourage in Cleveland and attended the funeral there. They afterward maintained a relationship with Lucretia Garfield, who returned to her home in Ohio.

Soon after the burial of President Garfield, Rutherford and Lucy went on a trip to New York City. With ever improving transportation, it took just twenty four hours on the train to get there. The purpose of the trip was to attend a meeting of the George Peabody Education Fund, for which Rutherford sat on the board of directors, and to have a portrait painted by William Merritt Chase for placement in the Harvard Memorial Hall.

"We are having a good time," Rutherford wrote back to Webb. "Our list of callers was never larger. Invitations are constantly coming."[6] Lucy was accompanied by friends in making a shopping and sightseeing tour of the city. "Your mother...is not fond of a great city," Rutherford wrote back to Fanny. "It is bewildering and the contrasts of condition between the prosperous and the unfortunate are painful to her."[7]

---

[6] Diary, October 6, 1881.
[7] Diary, October 9, 1881.

Lucy made a visit to Orange, New Jersey, to see Emma Foote Glenn, an old Cincinnati friend. When Lucy and her traveling companion returned to New York City after dark "the whole city was lighted by the burning of the large car stables a few squares from here," Rutherford wrote to Fanny. "Your mother, you know, is always greatly interested in the excitement and scenes of fires, and wanted me to go with her to this one, but I was in bed, the night was sharp, and I persuaded her to be content with seeing it from an upper window of the hotel."[8] They returned home after more than two weeks in the city.

They had a another delightful Christmas at the end of 1881. Rutherford enjoyed the crisp air and the sound of the waters in the nearby river. Webb brought many presents from Cleveland, and all the children except Rud made it home. Six days later Rutherford noted their 29th anniversary in his diary. "An event that gains with time," he commented.[9]

The ladies of Fremont made a banner for the local unit of the Grand Army of the Republic. On May 26, 1882, Lucy made a short speech to the group when it was presented, and it was accepted by a badly wounded veteran of the war. She and Rutherford attended aother reunion of the Army of the Potomac in Detroit in mid-June.

At the end of 1882 Lucy became involved with an elderly black woman by the name of Eliza, who had been one of her father's Kentucky slaves in the 1830s. Lucy felt they ought to support her in her old age, and Rutherford agreed. They invited her to come to Spiegel Grove and stay indefinitely, and sent fare for her transportation there.[10]

When Christmas came around again the entire family, including all three of the adult children, were able to gather in Spiegel Grove. Lucy had presents for all in the family, for everyone in the Sunday School class she taught, for each of the servants, and for many friends. "No holiday season was ever happier with us than this," Rutherford wrote in his diary. "Lucy has some symptoms of ill health which give us anxiety. But on the whole she is so strong, our children are so promising and good, that as a family we may deem ourselves peculiarly blessed."[11] Lucy held an open house on New Year's Day 1883 and received many callers.

On January 11th Rutherford and Lucy hosted yet another Grand Army of the Republic gathering of some two hundred people, this time held on the grounds of Spiegel Grove. There was a band and a glee club to sing patriotic songs. "Lucy with her usual tact and magnetic cheerfulness looked after the happiness of all

[8] Diary, October 11, 1881.
[9] Diary, December 30, 1881.
[10] Diary, late 1882.
[11] Diary, December 30, 1882.

until after nine o'clock," Rutherford wrote, "when she was compelled to leave by one of her severe and now too frequent colics. This she did so quietly that no one understood the cause. She found relief in about one hour."[12]

Like the fire in New York City, Lucy was fascinated by the destruction of "the greatest flood ever known at Fremont" in February of 1883. The rain began to freeze as it fell, making telegraph wires so heavy that they pulled the poles to be ground, or broke them. Small twigs became large, and a great many tree branches snapped from the weight. "For two or three hours the crash of falling limbs was almost constant. Even a small limb falling with its ice and the ice on other limbs which it broke would make a roaring noise," wrote Rutherford. "Lucy and the family watched the scene with the greatest interest. Many favorite trees were badly marred.... The losses that grieved us most are the injury to the large elm northeast of the house; one half of the tall sassafras; the tall young hickory in the orchard; the damage to three of the large old oaks, [and] to the four street elms."

The next day came the flooding. "Sunday was given up to the flood and the rescue and relief of the sufferers. No such flood was ever seen here before," Rutherford continued. "The water filled the valley from bluff to bluff. It ran two to four feet the whole length of Water Street, and drove from their homes perhaps one to three hundred families. Men in skiffs were at work all day Sunday, rescuing people. One woman was drowned - others perhaps.... The anecdotes of escapes, losses, and experiences are without number and often very interesting."[13]

In April of 1883 Rutherford was away when he received a dispatch from Rud that Lucy was very ill and that he should return at once. He did so. En route he received further word that she was now better, and on reaching Fremont found her completely recovered. She had been attacked by rheumatism or neuralgia of the stomach.

Christmas of 1883 was like the year before. Lucy had presents for all, including books such as "Swiss Family Robinson" to the twelve boys of her Sunday School class. She spent one day until eight in the evening at the new church, much of New Year's Day, until eight in the evening, at the new church, "making the Sunday [school] children happy with a Christmas tree donated by the Presbyterians. It was gay with candles, and stockings filled with candy, and festooned with strings of popcorn and cranberries. All a simple affair, but as happiness-giving as the more expensive affairs of the great cities."[14]

---

[12] Diary, January 11, 1883.
[13] Diary, February 4, 1883.
[14] Diary, January 1, 1884.

Lucy continued to mother her children by mail. The older boys were grown and working in other cities. "So my dear boy," she wrote to Rud, "remember the kind word and act towards the old and feeble or the poor and weak brings its own reward." She closed by saying "don't joke on religious matters and go to church for your mother's sake if nothing else."[15]

Fanny and Scott were boarded at schools in their teenage years. She tried to write them every week, and her letters were filled with motherly concern and advice. "Take the brightest and happiest views of life and strive always to be a sunbeam in the house," she wrote Fanny in 1883. "[W]hile cultivating all mental qualities do not forget the physical. Now you will smile - stand straight, throw your shoulders back, and walk erect."[16] Lucy gave some news of home, then enquired whether she had enough warm clothing for the winter.

"Your mother has serious regrets when she thinks how the dear daughter has been neglected by the Mama and Papa," she wrote Fanny in April of 1885. "Now my little darling we think of you early in the morning, pretty constantly though the day, at evening and all intervening hours of the dat and waking moments at night, but we are negligent about writing.... How much I desire your happiness, and so every little engagement or pleasure you have fills me with happiness, too."[17]

"And now may I write the little things," Lucy wrote to Scott, saying the things that mothers say best. "Be neat, don't forget to brush your teeth, your nails or blacking your shoes..... Now for important, very important, things. Be kind and courteous to your schoolmaster, polite and attentive to your teachers, avoid harsh and rude language. Don't take the boy for your friend that takes the name of God in vain. It is hardly necessary for me to say to you , avoid the saloon - don't enter one with a friend or for any purpose."[18]

Scott went to school in Ithaca, New York, and on a trip to Boston Lucy thought of stopping by to see him. "I did want to stop, or rather to go, to Ithaca to see you for a few hours," Lucy wrote him, "but feared you probably felt as your brothers did about the old lady coming to see them. So came directly home." She gave him her best counsel. "Have you anything pleasant or cheery in your room? For your mother's sake, don't neglect church, and my dear boy don't speak slighteningly of religion." As she wrote she again felt her own shortcomings. "I may not have been as careful as I should have been, and have noticed too much

---

[15] Letter Lucy to son Rutherford, dated November 19, 1881, Papers.
[16] Letter Lucy to Fanny, dated November 7, 1883, Papers.
[17] Letter Lucy to Fanny, dated April 1885, Papers.
[18] Letter Lucy to Scott, dated May 5, 1883, Papers.

the inconsistencies of professors of religion."[19] No one else would have made the criticism that Lucy Hayes was not as careful as she should have been.

Lucy continued to rebuff the efforts of Frances E. Willard to involve her in the Women's Christian Temperance Union. Lucy did, however, did consent to become involved in the Woman's Home Missionary Society of the Methodist Episcopal Church. This organization was dedicated to the helping and improving of the unhappy conditions of the poor in the United States, including recent immigrants. Her position was largely honorary, but she did lend her prestige to the cause, just as Rutherford did for his chosen organizations. In October of 1884 she and Rutherford went to Cleveland, where she presided over a meeting of the group. She resigned the presidency sometime in the late 1880s, saying that she continued to support the society's goals but that she had done her part as president.

In June of 1889 Rutherford was on his way home from a board meeting at Ohio State University in Columbus. Reaching home at about 5:30, Rud came to meet him. "He looked as if something awful was on his mind. We got into the carriage, when he said: 'I have very bad news for you,' and with sobs he told us that Lucy had an attack of paralysis about 4 o'clock," Rutherford wrote.

Rutherford explained in his diary what had happened. Lucy "was sitting in our room, first floor, in the bay, with Ella sewing. Ella noticed that Lucy had difficulty with her fingers trying to thread a needle; went over to her. Lucy could not speak. She was sitting in the large low chair that stands near the southeast window. She did not fall out of it at all, but sank back in it, and seemed to realize what had happened to her; was depressed and in tears."

Fanny was just outside the house, playing tennis with two friends. One of the tennis players, cousin Lucy Keeler, raced in a carriage to find a doctor, making people along the way wonder if her horse was a runaway. She brought back Dr. John, who spoke with Lucy. She was conscious but unable to speak. He had removed from chair and taken to her bed. When Rutherford arrived he thought Lucy knew him. She could not speak but seemed to pressed his hand in recognition.[20]

Word went out immediately to Fremont, and through telegraph wires to the nation, that Lucy Hayes had been stricken. Messages of encouragement poured in to Spiegel Grove from friends and strangers

Slowly Lucy slipped into unconsciousness, from which she never recovered. She was not able to speak any last words to anyone. The next day Dr. Rice with

---

[19] Letter Lucy to Scott, dated November 7, 1888, Papers.
[20] Diary, June 22, 1889.

difficulty aroused Lucy to take some medicine. It is easy to think of Rutherford, now 67 years old, thoughtfully sitting in a chair writing his thoughts in his diary, in a quiet home filled with concern. The family was all there. Her children were still fairly young. Birchard was 36 years old, Webb 33, Rutherford 31, Fanny 22 and Scott just 18. Fanny, when alone with her cousin Lucy Keeler, broke down and wept bitterly.

"The end is now inevitable. I can't realize it, but I think of her as gone," Rutherford wrote at 4:40 in the morning. "Dear, darling Lucy! When I saw and heard her last in full life, she was gathering flowers for me to carry to Mary, last Monday. When she found I would be too late for my train to Toledo if I waited longer, with her cheerful voice she said: 'Oh, well, it makes no difference. I can send them (or I will send them) by express at noon.' This she did, and Mary got them. I was barely in time for the train - not a moment to lose. A characteristic act. It was like her. For me the last - oh, the last! We wait. Letters and dispatches come from all quarters - full of words that sustain and encourage."[21]

The vigil went on all night. "All night her face was lovely, with a living warm beauty, and peaceful," wrote her niece Lucy Keeler wrote.[22] "It is past midnight, almost one o'clock. We do not expect Lucy to see the light of another day," Rutherford wrote. "All of our children, Birchard, Webb, Rutherford, Fanny, and Scott, are waiting for the inevitable close.... And Lucy herself is so sweet and lovely, as she lies unconsciously breathing away her precious life, that I feel a strange gratitude and happiness as I meditate on all the circumstances of this solemn transition we are waiting for.... It is indeed hard - hard indeed - to part with her."[23]

Lucy died at 6:30 a.m. on June 25, 1889 with her loving family around her. Rutherford held her hand, looking into her face, kissing her good-bye as she passed away. He then joined the children on the porch in the bracing air of a beautiful morning.[24]

Word of the passing of the former First Lady immediately went throughout the land. There was an outpouring of condolences from every corner of the country, so much so that Rutherford could not answer them. He prepared a printed sheet which he had sent to those he knew:

---

[21] Diary, June 24, 1889.
[22] "The Passing of Lucy Webb Hayes" by Lucy Elliott Keeler, Rutherford B. Hayes Presidential Center Library.
[23] Diary, June 25, 1889.
[24] Ibid.

The friends who have sent telegraphic messages, letters, floral tributes, and newspaper articles, tokens of their regard for Mrs. Hayes of sympathy for me and my family, are so numerous that I cannot, bu the use of pen alone, within the time it ought to be done, suitably express to all of them my gratitude and thanks. I therefore beg them to excuse me for sending in this form my assurance of the fullest appreciation of their kindness, and of my lasting and heartfelt obligation to each of them.

William H. Crook, his former White House staffer, received this card. At the bottom, in the President's handwriting, was added: "All your kind words find their way to my heart. Thankfully, Rutherford B. Hayes."[25]

A funeral service was held at Spiegel Grove on June 28, 1889. The minister Dr. L. D. McCabe, who had presided at their marriage in 1852, presided once again. As the hearse proceeded to the cemetery it was flanked by veterans of the 23rd Ohio.[26]

Lucy Webb Hayes was fortunate. She went from health to death without a period of physical or mental decline. Rutherford was shattered at her passing, but he carried on as best he could for three and a half more years in his philanthropic work. His last words were, "I know that I am going where Lucy is."[27]

---

[25] Crook, pp. 656-657.
[26] Geer, p. 273.
[27] Eckenrode, p. 341.

BIBLIOGRAPHY

Carl Sferraza Anthony, *First Ladies: The Saga of the Presidents' Wives and Their Power*, New York: William Morrow & Company, 1990.

Harry Bernard, *Rutherford B Hayes and his America*, New York: The Bobbs-Merrill Company, Inc., 1954.

Paul F. Boller, Jr., *Presidential Wives: An Anecdotal History*, New York: Oxford University Press, 1988.

Betty Boyd Caroli, *First Ladies*, New York: Oxford University Press, 1987.

William H. Crook, "Rutherford B. Hayes in the White House" in *The Century Magazine*, March 1909, Volume 77, No. 5.

Eliza Davis, *Lucy Webb Hayes: A Memorial Sketch*, Cincinnati: Cranston & Stowe, 1890.

Eliza Davis, *Lucy Webb Hayes: A Memorial Sketch*, Cincinnati: Woman's Home Missionary Society, 1892.

Kenneth E. Davison, *The Presidency of Rutherford B Hayes,* Westport, Connecticut: Greenwood Press, Inc., 1972.

William A. Degregorio, *The Complete Book of U.S. Presidents*, Fort Lee, New Jersey: Barricade Books, 2001.

H. J. Eckenrode, *Rutherford B. Hayes: Statesman of Reunion*, New York: Dodd, Mead & Company, 1930.

Edmund Fuller and David E. Green, *God in the White House: The Faiths of American Presidents*, New York: Crown Publishers, Inc., 1968.

Emily Apt Geer, *First Lady: The Life of Lucy Webb Hayes*, Fremont, Ohio: The utherford B. Hayes Presidential Center, 1995.

Lewis L. Gould, Editor, *American First Ladies: Their Lives and Their Legacy*, New York: Garland Publishing, Inc., 1996.

Margaret Harrington, "An Abstract of Lucy Webb Hayes as First Lady of the United States," Master thesis, Bowling Green State University, Bowling Green, Ohio, 1956.

Ari Hoogenboom, *The Presidency of Rutherford B Hayes*, Lawrence, Kansas: University Press of Kansas, 1988.

Ari Hoogdenboom, *Rutherford B Hayes: One of the Good Colonels*, Abilene, Texas: McWhiney Foundation Press, 1999.

Kathleen Prindiville, *First Ladies*, New York: The Macmillan Company, 1954.

Mrs. R. S. Rust, *Lucy Webb Hayes: A Memorial Sketch*, Cincinnati, Cranston & Stowe, 1890.

William Seale, *The President's House*, Washington, D.C.: The White House Historical Society, 1986.

Margaret Truman, *First Ladies,* New York: Random House, 1995.

Doug Wead, *All the President's Children*, New York: Atria Books, 2003.

Charles Richard Williams, Editor, *Diaries and Letters of Rutherford B. Hayes*, Columbus, Ohio: Ohio State Archeological and Historical Society, 1922.

John S. Wise, *Recollections of Thirteen Presidents*, Freeport, New York: Books for Libraries Press, 1968.

The Lucy Hayes Papers, Rutherford B. Hayes Presidential Center Library, Fremont, Ohio.